THIS BOOK

BELONGS TO

....

....

FARMHOUSE
RULES

FARMHOUSE RULES

RULES

SIMPLE, SEASONAL MEALS FOR THE WHOLE FAMILY

BY NANCY FULLER

Photographs by Jamie Prescott

GRAND CENTRAL
Life & Style
NEW YORK • BOSTON

Copyright © 2015 by Fuller Farmer, LLC

Photographs by Jamie Prescott

Grand Central Life & Style
Hachette Book Group
1290 Avenue of the Americas
New York, NY 10104

www.GrandCentralLifeandStyle.com

Printed in the United States of America

QMA

First Edition: October 2015

10 9 8 7 6 5 4 3 2 1

Grand Central Life & Style is an imprint of Grand Central Publishing.
The Grand Central Life & Style name and logo are trademarks of Hachette Book Group, Inc.

The Hachette Speakers Bureau provides a wide range of authors for speaking events.
To find out more, go to www.HachetteSpeakersBureau.com or call (866) 376-6591.

The publisher is not responsible for websites (or their content) that are not owned by the publisher.

Library of Congress Cataloging-in-Publication Data

Fuller, Nancy (Chef), author.
    Farmhouse rules : simple, seasonal meals for the whole family / by Nancy Fuller. — First edition.
        pages cm
    Includes index.
    ISBN 978-1-4555-3105-9 (hardcover)—ISBN 978-1-4555-3107-3 (ebook)   1. Cooking, American.
2. Seasonal cooking.   I. Title.
    TX715.F94 2015
    641.5973—dc23
                                                            2015025985

Design by Gary Tooth / Empire Design Studio

I am blessed.

This book is dedicated to my family.

And to everyone who has a family, is about to start a family, or is a part

of another's family, and to all the people who call me Gigi.

Contents

Gratitude

"THERE IS NO SINCERER LOVE THAN THE LOVE OF FOOD."
—GEORGE BERNARD SHAW

The group of people who came together to create this cookbook have shown an abundance of compassion, patience, and professionalism. I thank you.

To Jamie Prescott: You are exceptional. Your creative eye, your creative mind, and your flexibility and ability to find the farm in all that you shot are incomparable. I thank you.

To Kevin Provost: You are the most patient man I know. And fastidious. You did beautiful work. I thank you.

To Amy Stevenson: I'm indebted to you for interpreting my handful of flour, my pinch of salt, my basket of tomatoes, my bushel of corn, and my chop-chop-in-the-pot into teaspoons, tablespoons, cups, and oven temperatures so that my readers can replicate my wholesome meals. I thank you.

To Cyd McDowell: My mentor, my boss, my assistant, and then your real job, my food stylist. I thank you. I never trusted a skinny cook—until you!

To Kelly Nardin: Though short and sweet, you were fast and furious. I thank you.

To Christine Buckley: CeCe, your consistent motion and drive, in addition to your demeanor, did not go unnoticed. I thank you.

To Jeanne Lurvey: Always so competent, always so dear, always in order, always so demure. What a sense of style you have! I thank you. And to Ryan: Jeanne picked such a special guy to be her assistant in the world of props. Keep smiling! I thank you.

To Tessa Edick: You came through my farmhouse door to ask a question and popped out of my cornfield looking like Rita Hayworth. I thank you.

To Steve Carlis, Hank Norman, and 2 Market Media: Your insight was pretty impressive! For all your efforts on my behalf, I thank you.

To Deborah Schneider, my agent: You do what you do and you do it well! I thank you.

To Karen Murgolo, my editor from Grand Central Publishing Life & Style, who smiled at me from the moment we met: Throughout this adventure, you were so patient, so gracious, and never showed frustration or ire at my most naive questions. This book would not be published today without your expertise. I thank you.

To Gordon Elliott, Pasquale Defazio, and Jenny Kirsten: You know how to make a show great! I thank you.

To Betsy Miller and Diana Castaldini: For your constant support, your perception, your ability to write, your interpretation of my life, my thoughts, my written word, I thank you.

To Judy Whitbeck and Dena Pollack: Thank you for sharing your wonderful children.

To my family: The stories of our life together and the love that we share have been the impetus for this cookbook. I thank you.

To David Ginsberg: You are my biggest fan! I love you. And I love your resilience, for without it I would not be where I am today.

Introduction

I grew up an only child in a family of 12th-generation farmers, *Mayflower* descendants. My father was out of the house at 4 a.m. to milk the cows, clean the barn, plow the fields, and plant the corn and alfalfa on my family's 500-acre dairy farm in upstate New York. My mother and my grandmother Grammy Carl were the cooks. Grammy lived on her own farm just a few miles down the road. My earliest childhood memories include napping in a pile of hay and riding a tricycle up and down the center aisle of our cow barn while dodging squirts of milk from a cow. In preparation for milking, my father would pre-milk the cow by hand, squirting the milk into a strainer-topped cup to be certain the milk was clean. Later, Mother would put the milk in a glass bottle and let the cream rise to the top, scoop it into a bowl, add vanilla, a pinch of salt, and confectioners' sugar. She'd beat it until stiff, and voilà! We had fresh whipped cream for our summer strawberry shortcake. It was the epitome of seasonal, farm-to-table eating.

Growing up, I would help my mother and Grammy Carl shuck peas, pick green beans, and hull strawberries in the kitchen—all easy jobs that a child could do. While peeking out from behind Grammy Carl's apron strings, I learned that it took flour to make a cake, butter to make a really scrumptious fried egg, and that if you overcooked a piece of beef, it would be dry and tough. I watched her bake cakes, roast chickens, mash potatoes, and shape meat loaves, and when I was old enough, she taught me the fundamentals of cooking.

We made flavorful, comforting, seasonal dishes using food grown on our own land. I learned from an early age that produce was to be eaten at its seasonal peak. We always had fresh asparagus and peas in the spring, sweet corn and zucchini in the summer, potatoes and pumpkins in the fall, and squash in the winter, all from our garden. We also raised our own livestock. "Grass-fed, locally grown" meat was all I ever knew! Our steaks, rump roasts, and hamburgers came from our own animals—except on the days my father went out hunting for deer that roamed on our acreage and returned to make venison steaks.

Other early memories include learning to drive a Massey Ferguson tractor at about eight years old, if you can believe it. I would steer it as it drew hay wagons and the farmhands loaded and stacked freshly baled hay. I can still see my mother shouting at my father, "Jim, do *not* let that child drive that tractor!" But he did!

Then there was Johnny Dunn. He was our milk dumper, gardener, handyman, and in many ways, my nanny. I adored him. One day, Johnny decided to fertilize the lawn after fertilizing the garden, but he didn't tell my mother his plans. She had been planning a dinner party for that night and you can probably guess what happened next: By the time the guests arrived, the entire house reeked of cow manure. Thank goodness most of them were farmers and my mother had a soft spot for Johnny. Everyone had a good laugh!

Jokes and fun aside, everyone worked hard each and every day. And the fruits of our labor were displayed on our farmhouse dinner table every night, with meals featuring roast beef, meat loaf, chicken and dumplings, summer squash with tomatoes, Cheddar cheese, coleslaw, corn on the cob, baked beans, and homemade bread. The farm taught me the importance and value of food and cooking, while also instilling in me a strong work ethic.

More than that, growing up on a farm also taught me that the family table is where the family bond is created. In our chaotic grab-and-go culture on the run, we've lost touch with what it means to make a family meal, to eat together as a family. Aside from the obvious nutritional benefits, family meals give you the opportunity to share and communicate with your family in a meaningful way (dropping them off at school or soccer practice doesn't count!). Asking your children a simple question over dinner, such as "How was your day?"—and making sure they know you expect an answer—will go a long way in developing their communication skills.

To further your children's knowledge of food and make seasonal cooking a fun family activity, include your children in the preparation of meals. Take them to the farmers' market and let them decide which vegetable they want to buy and cook. This will not only teach them what quality food is, it will help them understand where their food comes from. Teach them that purchasing locally grown, seasonal food will ensure they get the freshest, healthiest ingredients available. Youngsters can also help create the week's menus, stir cake batter (my 37-year-old son still licks the beaters!), and clear the plates and silverware from the table at the end of a meal. These simple tasks will instill in them a work ethic that will carry them through the rest of their lives.

My first husband (now my *was-band*) was a dairy farmer, a true Renaissance man. He was a chemist (he knew how much fertilizer was needed for a certain amount of acreage); a veterinarian (he knew how to nurse a sick cow back to health); a horticulturist (he knew the science and art of planting); a mechanical engineer (he knew how to fix a tractor); a commodities analyst (he knew how much seed to buy each spring by analyzing the price of crops); and a nutritionist (he knew the amount of protein and fiber the cows needed to produce the correct amount of milk). Over time, he also became a psychologist: He was living with six females under one roof! I cooked the meals, and together we raised six children. The kitchen was the heart and soul of our farmhouse, and it took strength and tenacity to keep our family unit whole and connected. We ate together 7 days a week, 365 days a year.

Now I get to call many children my family—the children I raised, the people they married, and my grandchildren. I refer to them all as my kids (in no special order): Eleyce, Abigail, Sydney, Emma, Ian, Sarah, Bailey, Noah, John Fuller, Rachel, Isabella, Nita, Victoria, Sam, Miles, Ami, Lazaro, Tom, Kimberlee, Bill, Justin, Lorinda, Annie, Johnny, Jason, and Jeff. All of my children—the yours, the mine, the ours—have an appreciation of what they eat and of the meals they prepare (though some more so than others; all good things take time!).

Remember: Memories created at the table, one moment at a time, will be the glue that holds your family together. No one can take those memories from you. Hold them dear if you've made them. Work hard to create them if not. Surprise your family with a fancy dinner out of the blue, on a weeknight, for no reason. Even if the children don't remember, you will. And years down the line, you'll smile. I once made tournedos with béarnaise sauce (filet mignon with a fancy sauce) for my family on a school night, when we normally would've had something like baked chicken. My kids don't remember! But I remember creating that

memory. Something else I did when the kids were little, and still do today when I have the opportunity, was make my family their favorite recipes. My son John loves carrot cake. I'm still making carrot cake! Both my husband and was-band are very fond of rhubarb pie, and I'm finally getting pretty good at that one! One of my biggest accolades was the day I made an apple pie and my husband, David, said it was just like his mother's. I knew I had hit a home run.

My farming roots were an asset to my growing family, and they have since become even more than that: my future, my career, and what I represent to the viewers of my television show *Farmhouse Rules.* And with this book, I am bringing the very best of my farmhouse rules and values straight to your kitchen. The family dinner must be brought back to the table and it is my hope that the seasonal recipes, cooking tips, and mealtime etiquette in this book will help you do just that. What is more essential than food? Nothing. What is more fundamental than family? Nothing.

As we say on the farm, fresh is best (unless you're stressed) and it's always better with family.

After all, Farmhouse Rules!

Farmhouse Rules

for the Cook

Over the years, I have learned a thing or two about how to guarantee flavorful homemade food with minimal stress and mess in the kitchen. From the proper way to clean a cutting board to why it is imperative to preheat the oven, the tips, or "rules," I've compiled have saved me time and aggravation while ensuring that my food has the best texture and flavor.

Now I want to share them with you.

Knowing these simple tricks and techniques is often what makes the difference between a mediocre cook and a good cook. (For instance, pretty pot holders, though lovely, are often too thin; I've burned myself using them a few times!)

As you are cooking the recipes in this book, use these tips to keep your hands safe from burns, your fingers safe from cuts, your clothes clean, and your kitchen tools new. I hope they help you make dinner a premier event in the life of your family.

1. Always preheat the oven (well, except for one time, see page 9). If you want it at 450°F, preheating may take half an hour, so factor that in to your cooking time.

2. Bring most ingredients, such as meat, butter, and eggs, to room temperature before cooking them. This allows you to work more quickly; the butter will be pliable and the eggs will create more volume when beaten.

3. Wear an apron. It will save you money on dry cleaning.

4. Use thick pot holders. Thin ones will burn you.

5. Keep a tasting spoon handy, and use it. Don't depend on the recipe to be foolproof; the strength of an herb's flavor may vary and oven temperatures always vary. As do taste buds.

6. Use a rubber spatula. It will get all the batter out of the bowl. Waste not, want not.

7. Always use a wooden spoon. Except on scrambled eggs; they'll stick.

8. Use sharp knives. They won't cut you—in fact, if you use a dull knife, you'll be more likely to cut yourself.

9. Always use a meat thermometer. You don't want to overcook a really expensive piece of meat.

10. Purchase spices in small amounts. They don't last forever.

11. Never submerge a wooden spoon or cutting board in water—it will dry out and break. That means no dishwashers! Instead, use soap and a sponge to wipe it down, and dry it immediately.

12. Don't leave a cast-iron skillet in water—it will rust. Rinse and dry it immediately.

13. While in the kitchen, clean up as you go—unless you have human dishwashers running around.

14. Set up and prep all the ingredients before you begin cooking your recipe.

15. Always read the recipe through from beginning to end.

Farmhouse Wares
for the Cook

ᘛ⬤

HAPPY HOMEMAKER, HAPPY WIFE, HAPPY LIFE.

The unglamorous and glamorous list of must-haves! You may not want or need all the items on this list, but whether you're an experienced cook or a beginner, it helps to have this equipment around when you have an impulse to whip up something scrumptious after being inspired by your favorite Food Network show. (Preferably *Farmhouse Rules!*)

Digital instant-read thermometer

Candy/jelly/fryer thermometer

Heavy Dutch oven pot

Cast-iron skillet

Skillet just for eggs

Muffin tin

Cake pans

Pie plate

Baking sheet/cookie sheet

Stainless-steel bowls

Wire rack that fits in rimmed baking sheet

Food processor

Wooden spoon

Slotted spoon

Scissors

Tongs

Spatula

Vegetable peeler

Strainer

Lettuce spinner

Box grater

Measuring cups

Measuring spoons

Spaghetti prongs

Corkscrew

Bottle opener

Timer

Candlesticks

Candles

Place mats

Cloth napkins

Farmhouse Rules cookbook

Thoughts on Cooking
Before You Start

At the turn of the twentieth century, recipes were called "rules." This book was designed to be an easy read with a group of core rules, or recipes, for each season. You will find one breakfast recipe each in spring, summer, fall, and winter to bid you a good morning and a good start to your day. You will then find recipes for lunches, starters, and sides, including soups and salads, and an hors d'oeuvre or two. Next, you will find supper dishes, usually the most important meal of the day; and finally, some seasonal desserts.

Remember to be creative and use your favorite fruits and vegetables, especially if you don't care for the ones I've chosen.

In order to eat seasonally year-round, remember to buy freezer bags and throw in fresh fruits and vegetables from each season to keep in the freezer. If you go berry picking, pick extra and freeze them so you can enjoy blueberry pancakes on a snow day.

Remember to always taste as you cook because our taste buds are all different. You might like more garlic than I do. If so, taste the dish and add more.

All ovens vary in their temperature and that is why I tell you to use a digital thermometer. It's better than being disappointed by a dried-out cake or roast.

The most important rule I have is to try these recipes and if one fails, try it again! Tweak my recipes to create your own. Discover the fun you can have.

"GOOD COOKS ARE BORN,
THEY SAY
THE SAYING IS MOST TRUE
AN EASY READ OF THESE RULES
WILL MAKE GOOD COOKS OF YOU!"
—ANONYMOUS

SPRING

Chapter 1

*How technology has blossomed. I remember when we
watered the garden with buckets! Now look at the
water tanks that automatically water as we plant.*

SPRING RECIPES

In the spring, farmers sow (another word for plant) what they will reap in the fall. In the Northeast, May is the month we begin planting. Before that, we plow and harrow the fields to cultivate the soil, and pick rock, which is when we collect loose stones from the dirt to ready the soil.

My childhood on the farm taught me what foods were in season and how to prepare them—knowledge I passed along to my own kids. When I was growing up, my mother and I would go on scavenger hunts to find fiddlehead ferns in the woods near our home, and now I do this with my grandchildren. A sure sign of spring, fiddleheads shoot up in wild, wet, and swampy areas in April, so searching for them always takes you off the beaten track. When you get back to the house, you soak them in water, their little brown skins come off, and you're left with this beautiful green pinwheel. My mother and Grammy Carl would cook them simply in olive oil or butter and add salt and pepper. Dandelion greens are another vegetable that grows wild in the spring. Grammy Carl would drizzle the cooked greens with a little maple syrup to get me to eat them. Try this with your kids at home. Though they are bitter, they cleanse the liver!

Spring is also the season when chickens naturally lay more eggs. When my children were growing up, we would color eggs for Easter and then I'd have tons of leftover eggs that I didn't know what to do with! So, for weeks, we'd have hard-boiled or deviled eggs for breakfast and snacks, lots of egg salad, and spinach salad with chopped hard-boiled eggs on top. Now I realize why my grandmother Fuller always had eggshell dolls in the spring! She'd blow out the contents of the eggs and we'd paint faces on them, make hats out of fabric, and make a collar that the egg would sit on.

The spring months are also the perfect time to cook lamb and trout. As a child, I used to pick fresh mint along the streams near our farm so that Grammy Carl could make mint jelly to serve with the lamb. And there was a brook and a pond across the road where I would use my bamboo pole to fish for trout (but I never brought dinner home!).

The vibrant spring recipes in the following pages showcase delicious, freshly harvested seasonal vegetables such as crisp asparagus, sweet peas, and colorful radishes and rhubarb. And the delectable roasts and fish dishes make great centerpieces for your Easter or Passover meal, or even a warm-weather weeknight meal.

Overnight Totally Tasty
French Toast

SERVES A LOT OF KIDS, OR 10 TODDLERS AND 4 PARENTS

12 large eggs

2 cups milk

1 cup heavy cream

½ cup (1 stick) salted butter, melted

1 tablespoon vanilla extract

1 tablespoon ground cinnamon

Pinch salt

1 cup maple syrup

1 loaf challah bread, sliced

This is a great recipe for a crowd. And it's the perfect answer when all my grandbabies run downstairs and ask, "What's for breakfast?"

The combination of sweet and savory flavors is a delicious and easy way to get children to eat the protein they need to make their bodies and minds function properly. Breakfast is the most important meal of the day and it should be the largest meal as well. It starts your engine running!

MIX TOGETHER the eggs, milk, cream, butter, vanilla, cinnamon, and salt in a medium bowl. Pour the maple syrup into the bottom of a 9- by 15-inch baking dish. Place the slices of bread on top of the maple syrup, tightly placing them next to each other. Pour the egg mixture on top. Cover and refrigerate overnight.

In the morning, turn the oven on to 350°F. (This is one recipe where it's not necessary to preheat the oven. Especially if you're just getting out of bed and need to rush in and get the French toast in the oven early before you hear the patter of bare feet!) Put the French toast in the oven and bake for 1 hour and 15 minutes. It's done when you see a lovely brown toasty topping. And the fragrance fills the air.

"ALL HAPPINESS DEPENDS ON A LEISURELY BREAKFAST."
—JOHN GUNTHER

Salmon Salad Sandwiches

SERVES 4

2 tablespoons mayonnaise

1 tablespoon Dijon mustard

1 tablespoon extra-virgin olive oil

Grated zest and juice of ½ lemon

½ teaspoon dried dill

¼ teaspoon granulated onion

Kosher salt

Freshly ground black pepper to taste

1 pound leftover cooked salmon
(such as Upriver Salmon, page 252)

½ cup chopped celery

¼ cup chopped cornichons or gherkins
(but not sweet gherkins, you want sour here)

8 slices multigrain bread, lightly toasted

½ cup thinly sliced English or other
seedless cucumber

2 big handfuls baby arugula

When you make salmon for dinner, be sure to make extra so you have leftovers for these tasty sandwiches. Whenever I buy a side of salmon (which usually weighs about 3 pounds), I poach it to enjoy with a mayo and Dijon mustard sauce for the first meal, flake it over greens for a second meal, and, last but not least, I make salmon salad for the third meal.

This recipe comes down to me through my grammy Tabor. She raised five kids and was the queen of leftovers.

IN A LARGE BOWL, stir together the mayonnaise, mustard, olive oil, lemon zest and juice, dried dill, granulated onion, and some salt and pepper. Flake in the salmon in large chunks and add the celery and cornichons. Toss gently with a fork, just to lightly dress the salmon without breaking it up too much. Refrigerate for 30 minutes.

Lay out 4 slices of bread and top each with the sliced cucumbers, a scoop of salmon salad, and some arugula. Top with the remaining bread and cut each sandwich in half with a serrated knife.

Spring Salad with Goat Cheese

SERVES 6

"EATING IS AN AGRICULTURAL ACT."
—WENDELL BERRY

12 slices baguette or walnut bread

Kosher salt

Freshly ground black pepper

2 cups sugar snap peas, trimmed
and halved crosswise

6 tablespoons extra-virgin olive oil,
plus more for brushing the bread

2 tablespoons balsamic vinegar

2 tablespoons chopped fresh chives

2 cups quartered strawberries

1 (5-ounce) log fresh goat cheese

12 cups fresh baby spring greens
(spinach, arugula, and romaine)

¼ cup toasted salted sunflower seeds

My favorite cheese is goat cheese and my long-time friend Anne Bossi, an award-winning cheese maker from Maine, often sends me samples—but not often enough! This recipe allows me to use as little or as much goat cheese as my taste buds desire. Or as much as Anne has sent!

Sweet spring berries are a nice contrast to the tart goat cheese. As is, the salad makes a lovely spring lunch. Add a little cooked chicken and you have a main course for dinner. And, as always, it's easy! Maybe someday I'll tell you how I almost burned down Anne's kitchen… almost!

PREHEAT THE OVEN to 400°F. Bring a medium saucepan of salted water to a boil. Arrange the bread slices on a baking sheet and toast them in the oven until crisp, 5 to 7 minutes. Brush the bread lightly with olive oil while still warm and season with salt and pepper. Set aside.

Add the snap peas to the boiling water and cook until crisp-tender, 2 to 3 minutes. Drain and rinse under cold water. Pat dry.

In a large bowl, whisk together the 6 tablespoons olive oil, vinegar, chives, and some salt and pepper. Add the quartered strawberries and let sit a minute while you get the rest of the salad together.

Spread a chunk of goat cheese on each baguette slice.

Add the snap peas and greens to the strawberries and season with salt and pepper. Place the salad on individual serving plates. Add 2 goat cheese toasts to each plate, sprinkle with the sunflower seeds, and serve.

Lawn Chicken Salad

SERVES 4 TO 6

2 bone-in, skin-on chicken breasts (about 1½ pounds)

3 cloves garlic, smashed and peeled

¼ cup buttermilk

2 tablespoons mayonnaise

2 tablespoons cider vinegar

2 tablespoons extra-virgin olive oil

2 teaspoons honey

1 teaspoon curry powder

½ teaspoon cumin

Kosher salt

Freshly ground black pepper

¼ cup chopped fresh chives

10 cups mixed baby greens (arugula, baby spinach, baby kale, baby romaine, etc.)

½ English cucumber, diced

1 ripe avocado, halved, seeded, and diced

½ cup thinly sliced radishes

½ cup slivered almonds, toasted

½ cup chopped dried apricots

Everyone loves chicken. My family is no exception! This is the perfect dish for a picnic indoors or outdoors, in the kitchen or the backyard, when the weather warms up. This recipe name is a nod to free-range chickens, who roam free on grassy land.

If you use leftover chicken, you'll need 2 to 2½ cups chunked chicken.

PUT THE CHICKEN BREASTS, skin side up, in a pot just large enough to hold them. Add enough water to cover the chicken by 2 inches and drop in the garlic cloves. Bring the water to a gentle simmer and cook until the chicken is just cooked through, about 25 minutes. Turn off the heat and let the chicken cool in the poaching liquid.

Drain the chicken (you can save the poaching liquid for a soup stock). Remove the skin and bones and chop or tear the meat into small chunks.

In a small bowl, whisk together the buttermilk, mayonnaise, vinegar, olive oil, honey, curry powder, and cumin. Season with salt and pepper and stir in the chives. Refrigerate while you assemble the rest of the salad.

Place the greens on a large platter and top with the chicken, cucumber, avocado, radishes, almonds, and apricots. Drizzle the dressing over the salad and season with salt and pepper.

Spring Fling Fiddlehead Soup
with Caramelized-Onion Sour Cream

SERVES 6

2 tablespoons unsalted butter

2 tablespoons extra-virgin olive oil

1 large yellow onion, thinly sliced

Pinch sugar

Kosher salt

Freshly ground black pepper

2 tablespoons all-purpose flour

2 teaspoons chopped fresh thyme

3 cups coarsely chopped fiddleheads (washed and trimmed)

1 quart low-sodium chicken broth

¾ cup sour cream

1 to 2 tablespoons milk, for thinning the sour cream

When I was a child, my mother and I would search for fiddlehead ferns, a wild vegetable that grows in moist woodland areas. To clean fiddlehead ferns, trim away any black or soft spots. The slight covering of brown paper–like skin will easily come off when you swish the fiddlehead ferns around in cold water. Repeat once or twice more, until clean. Fiddleheads have a short season. If you miss them, or live somewhere where you can't get them, try substituting fresh asparagus. Both of these great spring vegetables have so many nutritious, cleansing qualities after the long winter.

IN A LARGE SAUCEPAN, melt the butter in the olive oil over medium heat. Add the onions and season with the sugar, salt, and pepper. Cook, stirring frequently, until they are a deep golden color, about 15 minutes. You may have to adjust the heat while you cook so they don't burn. With tongs, remove half of the onions to a small bowl and reserve.

Add the flour and thyme to the onion in the saucepan and cook, stirring, for a minute. Add the fiddleheads and broth. Bring to a simmer and cook until the fiddleheads are very tender, 10 to 15 minutes. Season with salt and pepper.

Puree the soup with ½ cup of the sour cream in batches in a blender (or with a handheld immersion blender right in the pot). Thin the remaining ¼ cup sour cream with 1 to 2 tablespoons milk, to the consistency of heavy cream.

To serve, ladle the soup into warmed soup bowls. Drizzle each serving with some of the sour cream and swirl in some of the reserved caramelized onions.

Orzo Salad with Spring Peas
and Creamy Herb Dressing

SERVES 4

12 ounces orzo

Kosher salt

2 cups fresh shelled (or frozen) peas

8 ounces sugar snap peas, trimmed and halved crosswise (about 1½ cups)

¼ cup buttermilk

¼ cup mayonnaise

Grated zest and juice of 1 lemon

¼ cup extra-virgin olive oil

½ cup chopped fresh chives

¼ cup chopped fresh Italian parsley

¼ cup chopped fresh dill

Freshly ground black pepper

This is a great, simple dish to make in the spring, or any time of year really—just swap in whatever vegetables are in season. Make it with winter squash in the fall, or add basil, mint, or cilantro for a summer version.

I frequently cook with orzo because it's my husband David's favorite. But rather than use butter and cheese, his favorites as well, I make this salad with buttermilk for a lighter, less-caloric dish.

BRING A LARGE POT of salted water to a boil. Add the orzo and boil for 5 minutes. Add the peas and boil for 3 minutes more. Finally, add the sugar snap peas and cook until the sugar snap peas and the orzo are just tender, 2 to 3 minutes more. Drain and rinse the orzo and vegetables under cold water to stop the cooking. Drain well and transfer the orzo and vegetables to a large bowl.

In a small bowl, stir together the buttermilk, mayonnaise, and lemon zest and juice. Whisk in the olive oil to make a smooth dressing, then stir in the herbs.

Drizzle the dressing over the orzo and toss well. Season with salt and pepper and serve. The salad can also be made earlier in the day and refrigerated, though you may need to loosen it up with a bit of buttermilk before serving.

Carefree Crab
and Horseradish Bake

SERVES 6 TO 8

8 ounces block cream cheese, softened

1 cup (4 ounces) shredded sharp white Cheddar cheese

½ cup mayonnaise

¼ cup prepared horseradish, drained

1 teaspoon Old Bay seasoning

1 tablespoon lemon juice

8 ounces crabmeat, picked over for shells

¼ cup chopped scallions

¼ cup chopped red bell pepper

½ cup finely crushed butter crackers (such as Ritz), plus more for serving

1 tablespoon unsalted butter, melted

This dip is a crowd favorite, especially among the football and basketball enthusiasts who like to eat while they holler and hoot.

If you can't find fresh crabmeat or don't want to spend the money on it, you can use surimi (imitation crab, made from cod), which is just as delicious.

PREHEAT THE OVEN to 400°F. In a large bowl, mix together the cream cheese, Cheddar cheese, mayonnaise, horseradish, and Old Bay until relatively smooth. Sprinkle with the lemon juice, add the crab, and gently fold it in. Stir in the scallions and bell pepper until just combined.

Spread the mixture in a 1-quart oval baking dish. In a small bowl, toss the cracker crumbs with the melted butter and sprinkle over the top of the baking dish. Bake until brown and bubbly, 15 to 17 minutes. Serve with crackers.

Edna's Easy
Homemade Salsa

MAKES ABOUT 1½ CUPS

4 plum tomatoes, cut into quarters, seeds removed

½ cup fresh cilantro leaves

¼ red onion, cut into chunks

1 clove garlic, smashed and peeled

1 jalapeño, stemmed, seeds removed, quartered

Juice of 1 lime

Kosher salt

Freshly ground black pepper

A viewer saw me make this recipe on TV and wrote me asking, "Why do I buy salsa, when this is *so* easy to make?" That's exactly my message!

I include "Edna" in the recipe name because it is Grammy Carl's first name and her love and support made me who I am today.

COMBINE THE TOMATOES, cilantro, onion, garlic, jalapeño, lime juice, and some salt and pepper in the bowl of a food processor and pulse until blended together. You want the salsa to maintain some texture, but it should still be smoother than it would be if you were chopping by hand. Pour into a bowl and serve. The salsa will also keep, covered, in the refrigerator for several days, though the flavors will get stronger.

THE QUALITY OF FOOD AND THE FRESHNESS OF FOOD AFFECT THE FLAVOR AND OUTCOME OF THE DISH.

Perfect Roasted Red Peppers

SERVES 4

3 medium red bell peppers
(or 1 each red, yellow, and orange)

12 anchovy fillets

12 fresh basil leaves

12 fresh mozzarella bocconcini (balls)

Kosher salt

Freshly ground black pepper

4 tablespoons extra-virgin olive oil
(plus more for the baking sheet)

8 cups mixed baby greens

2 tablespoons balsamic vinegar

4 slices toasted or grilled country bread

An appetizer at one of my favorite restaurants, Il Girasole in Delray Beach, Florida, inspired this recipe.

While this can be served as an appetizer or a side dish, it also works as an hors d'oeuvre if made with smaller slices of crusty, toasted country bread and smaller pieces of pepper and mozzarella.

PREHEAT THE OVEN to 450°F with a rack in the top third.

Char the peppers over an open burner flame on high until blackened on all sides, or cut them in half and place them on a baking sheet, pulp side down, and roast in the 450°F oven for 20 minutes. Put in a large bowl, cover tightly with plastic wrap, and allow the peppers to cool completely. Peel off the skins, rinsing the peppers if necessary to get them completely clean.

Cut out the stems, then halve the peppers through the tops. Clean out the ribs and seeds, then halve the peppers again through the tops, to get 4 quarters from each of the 3 peppers. You should have 12 pieces in all.

Brush a rimmed baking sheet with olive oil. Arrange the peppers in rows, ribbed side up, on the baking sheet. Layer an anchovy over each pepper strip, then add a basil leaf. Place a mozzarella ball in the center of each. Season with salt and pepper. Roll up each pepper piece and secure with a toothpick. Drizzle the peppers with 2 tablespoons of the olive oil. Bake until the peppers are heated through and the cheese just begins to melt but still holds its shape, about 5 minutes.

To serve, place the greens on 4 plates. Put 3 pepper purses on top of each salad. Drizzle the greens with the remaining 2 tablespoons olive oil and the balsamic vinegar and season with salt and pepper. Serve with slices of grilled or toasted country bread to sop up the juices.

Roasted Asparagus
with Cheesy Crumbs

SERVES 4 TO 6

2 bunches asparagus (medium thickness), about 2 pounds total

3 tablespoons extra-virgin olive oil

6 leafy sprigs fresh thyme

Kosher salt

Freshly ground black pepper

¼ cup grated Parmesan cheese

This is an easy and delicious way to serve asparagus when it's in season. The roasting really concentrates its flavor. It's tasty served warm or at room temperature and any leftovers are great the next day, chopped up in a salad or added to scrambled eggs. The best news? One stalk of asparagus has only 3 calories—and loads of fiber.

PREHEAT THE OVEN to 450°F with a rimmed baking sheet on the bottom rack. Trim any woody bases from the bottom of the asparagus.

Remove the heated baking sheet from the oven. Roll the asparagus onto the baking sheet and drizzle with the olive oil. Add the thyme sprigs and give everything a toss so the asparagus is coated with oil. Make sure the asparagus land in one layer. Season with salt and pepper. Roast until the asparagus is almost tender, 12 to 13 minutes.

Give the asparagus a toss and gather them together in an even layer. Switch your oven to broil. Sprinkle the asparagus with the Parmesan and roast on the top rack until the cheese is crisp and crusty and the asparagus are browned and tender, 1 to 2 minutes, depending on your broiler.

Buttery Braised Radishes

SERVES 4 TO 6

5 tablespoons unsalted butter

3 bunches radishes with tops
(see instructions below)

1 bunch scallions, cut into ½-inch lengths
(about 1½ cups)

1 cup low-sodium chicken broth or water

1 teaspoon sugar

Kosher salt

Freshly ground black pepper

1 tablespoon red wine vinegar

2 tablespoons chopped fresh
mint leaves

When you are shopping, try to buy radishes with the tops still attached. Most people don't think of eating the tops, but they have a nice peppery flavor and cook in no time at all. Wash the radishes and tops well and trim all but about ½ inch of the tops from the bulbs. If you're using the larger globe radishes, halve them. If you can find small, slender breakfast radishes, you can braise them whole, but buy an extra bunch since they're smaller.

HEAT A LARGE SKILLET over medium heat. Add 3 tablespoons of the butter and when it melts, add the radishes and scallions and toss to coat in the butter. Add the broth and sugar and season with salt and pepper. Scatter the radish tops over the mixture and dot with the remaining 2 tablespoons butter. Bring to a simmer, cover, and cook until radishes and tops are tender but still firm, about 10 minutes. You should still feel some resistance when you poke them with a fork.

Uncover, and use tongs to remove the tops to a serving plate. Add the vinegar to the skillet and bring to a boil. Cook, tossing frequently, until the sauce is reduced to a glaze, about 1 minute. Sprinkle with the mint, stir, and serve on the bed of radish greens.

Maple Syrup–Mustard Glazed
Turkey Breast

SERVES 6, WITH LEFTOVERS

BRINE AND TURKEY

2 cups apple cider

½ cup maple syrup

½ bunch fresh thyme sprigs

2 bay leaves

½ cup kosher salt

1 orange, cut into quarters

1 whole bone-in, skin-on turkey breast
(about 5 pounds)

SPICE RUB AND GLAZE

2 tablespoons unsalted butter

1 teaspoon paprika

½ teaspoon dry mustard

½ teaspoon dried sage

¼ teaspoon granulated garlic

¼ teaspoon freshly ground black pepper

¼ cup maple syrup

2 tablespoons Dijon mustard

One of the best tricks I learned when I worked as a caterer was to roast a large turkey breast instead of a whole turkey. A whole turkey has too many components that I can't use, and a breast requires less cooking time. When my kids were growing up, I always roasted a larger piece than dinner called for so I had turkey sandwiches for school lunches during the week.

Take the time to brine—it's worth it. It's easy, and it keeps the meat moist.

FOR THE BRINE, in a pot large enough to hold the turkey breast comfortably, combine 2 quarts water with the cider, maple syrup, thyme, bay leaves, salt, and orange quarters. Bring to just a simmer. Add 2 quarts ice water (about half ice/half water). Let come to room temperature. Submerge the turkey in the brine, cover, and refrigerate overnight or all day (about 12 hours).

To season, roast, and glaze the turkey, preheat the oven to 400°F. Arrange a rack in a large roasting pan (a V-shaped roasting rack is ideal, but if you don't have that, any rack is fine).

Remove the turkey from the brine, rinse well, and pat dry. Loosen the skin of the turkey breast with your fingers and rub the butter under the breast. In a small bowl, stir together the paprika, dry mustard, sage, granulated garlic, and pepper and rub all over the turkey breast. Set the turkey on the rack breast side up and roast for 30 minutes.

Meanwhile, in a small bowl, stir together the maple syrup and mustard. After 30 minutes, reduce the oven temperature to 325°F and brush the turkey with some of the glaze. Continue to roast, basting twice more, until a meat thermometer inserted into the thickest part of the breast reads 165°F, about 1½ hours, depending on the size of the breast. Let the turkey rest on a cutting board for 15 minutes before carving.

Divine Chicken Divan

SERVES 6

Kosher salt

1 large head broccoli, cut into 1- to 2-inch florets, tender stems peeled and cut into ½-inch slices (about 5 cups)

5 tablespoons unsalted butter (plus more for the casserole)

1 tablespoon chopped fresh sage

5 tablespoons all-purpose flour

3 tablespoons dry sherry

1 cup low-sodium chicken broth

1 cup milk

1 cup heavy cream

Pinch freshly grated nutmeg

Freshly ground black pepper

1 bunch scallions, chopped (about 1 cup)

1½ cups (6 ounces) shredded Gruyère cheese

1 cooked chicken (or leftover turkey meat), meat removed and cut into chunks, skin and bones discarded (3 to 3½ cups meat)

½ cup sliced or slivered almonds, toasted

½ cup grated Parmesan cheese

¼ cup breadcrumbs

This is an old favorite in our home. The sherry is what makes this a "classic" chicken divan, but if you don't have any on hand feel free to use a splash of white wine (or omit the alcohol altogether). Everyone goes crazy for this dish—even the barn animals! One day before a friend's dinner party, I put a large ceramic dish of chicken divan on the outside porch and then went back inside to get dressed. After a big rumble and crash, there was no more chicken divan! The barn cats had found it and eaten every last bit by the time I ran outside to see what had happened.

PREHEAT THE OVEN to 400°F and butter a shallow 3-quart casserole dish. Bring a large saucepan of salted water to a boil. Add the broccoli and cook until bright green and almost tender (you still want it to have a little bite, it will cook more in the oven). Cool under cold running water and pat very dry. Set aside.

In a large saucepan, melt 4 tablespoons of the butter over medium heat. When the butter is melted, add the sage and let sizzle a minute, then add the flour. Cook the roux (or else it will taste like raw flour), whisking, for about 3 minutes, without letting it brown. Pour in the sherry and cook to reduce it away, about 1 minute. Whisk in the broth, milk, cream, and nutmeg and season with salt and pepper. Bring to a simmer and cook, whisking occasionally to get out any lumps, until thickened, 6 to 7 minutes. Stir in the scallions and Gruyère until the cheese is melted, then remove the sauce from the heat.

In a large bowl, mix together the sauce, broccoli, chicken, and almonds until thoroughly coated. Pour into the prepared casserole dish. In a small bowl, melt the remaining 1 tablespoon butter in the microwave, then toss with the Parmesan and breadcrumbs. Sprinkle the mixture over the top of the casserole. Bake until browned and bubbling, about 35 minutes.

"THE SHARED MEAL ELEVATES EATING FROM
A MECHANICAL PROCESS OF FUELING THE BODY TO A
RITUAL OF FAMILY AND COMMUNITY."
—MICHAEL POLLAN

Chop-Chop-in-the-Pot
Roast Chicken

SERVES 4

1 (5-pound) roasting chicken

Kosher salt

Freshly ground black pepper

4 tablespoons unsalted butter, softened

6 sprigs fresh sage

3 onions, peeled and quartered

4 large carrots, cut into chunks

4 stalks celery, cut into chunks

½ cup white wine

1 teaspoon pepper

2 teaspoons salt

2 teaspoons paprika

2 teaspoons granulated garlic

2 teaspoons granulated onion

This has been my go-to roast chicken forever, and everyone loves it. My best friend Betsy will call and ask when I'm making roast chicken, or if I invite her for dinner, she will ask me to make it. This recipe is a chop-chop-in-the-pot, meaning the vegetables are chunked, thrown in the pot with the chicken, and you're done! Easy.

If you have some time before roasting the chicken, season it with the spices and salt and let it sit, uncovered, in the fridge for a few hours. This will infuse the chicken with the spices and dry out the skin a bit so it's nice and crisp once roasted.

PREHEAT THE OVEN to 400°F.

Rinse the inside of the chicken and season with salt and pepper, inside and out. Rub the softened butter all over the chicken and under the skin of the breast. Stuff the cavity with the sage. In the bottom of the pot, add the onions, carrots, and celery. Set the chicken on top of the vegetables and pour in the wine. Sprinkle on top of the chicken the pepper, salt, paprika, granulated garlic, and granulated onion. Roast for 2 hours. If you're not sure it's done, put a thermometer in the thickest part of the chicken (the thigh); it should read 165°F. Remove the chicken to a cutting board to rest for 10 minutes.

Place the chicken on a platter. Remove the vegetables from the pan and arrange around the chicken. Pour the pan juices into a measuring cup, let them settle, and spoon off the fat. Pour the juices over the chicken and vegetables and serve.

Farmer's Fish Stew

SERVES 6

2 tablespoons unsalted butter

4 ounces slab bacon, diced

1 medium onion, chopped

3 stalks celery, chopped

1 tablespoon chopped fresh thyme

1 clove garlic, chopped

3 tablespoons all-purpose flour

2 bay leaves

1 cup bottled clam juice

1 quart low-sodium chicken broth

1 cup heavy cream

1 pound Yukon gold potatoes, cut into
1-inch chunks

12 ounces skinless firm white fish fillets,
such as halibut, swordfish, or cod

18 small littleneck clams (or manila clams)

8 ounces peeled and deveined medium shrimp

8 ounces bay scallops (or sea scallops, halved)

¼ cup chopped fresh Italian parsley

Grilled or toasted country bread slices,
for serving

On my childhood farm, Johnny Dunn, our live-in all-around handyman, was my nanny and babysitter, the milk dumper, and the gardener. And he was Catholic, so he couldn't have meat on Fridays. Keeping that in mind, my mother would make fish stew for dinner for all of us, and we loved it.

I use cod or another hearty white fish only; other fish will be too fragile and fall apart or disappear in the pot. And don't buy anything too strongly flavored, like bluefish.

MELT THE BUTTER in a large Dutch oven over medium heat. Add the bacon and cook until crisp, then remove to a paper towel–lined plate to drain.

Add the onion and celery to the pan and cook in the leftover bacon fat until softened, about 8 minutes. Add the thyme and garlic and cook until fragrant, about 1 minute. Add the flour and cook, stirring, for 1 minute. Add the bay leaves, clam juice, chicken broth, and cream. Bring to a simmer and add the potatoes. Cover and simmer until the potatoes are just tender, 8 to 10 minutes.

Add the fish to the pan, then the clams. Cover the pot and simmer until some of the clams begin to open, about 4 minutes. Drop the shrimp and scallops into the pot and cover again. Simmer until all of the clams have opened (discarding any that don't) and the fish, shrimp, and scallops are just cooked through, about 4 minutes. Discard the bay leaves. Top with parsley and crumbled bacon and serve with warm country bread.

Bacon-Wrapped Trout

SERVES 2

2 (8-ounce) rainbow trout, cleaned and butterflied

Kosher salt

Freshly ground black pepper

2 tablespoons extra-virgin olive oil

2 tablespoons chopped fresh herbs, such as parsley, chives, and thyme

1 tablespoon capers, drained and chopped

2 cloves garlic, finely chopped

Juice of ½ lemon, plus 4 thin lemon slices

4 slices bacon

This was a popular recipe from the *Farmhouse Rules* episode where my friend Pam and I went fishing. Though it was fishing season when we filmed, it was early spring and the creek waters were still rushing—and as every fisherman knows, you can't easily catch a trout in rapid running water. So we took frozen fish, hooked them on the lines, and made them wiggle through the water by wiggling our fishing poles. The magic of television!

PREHEAT THE OVEN to 425°F. Sprinkle the inside and outside of each trout with salt and pepper. Combine 1 tablespoon of the olive oil, the herbs, capers, garlic, lemon juice, and some salt and pepper in a small bowl and divide this mixture between the insides of the two trout. Fold the trout back onto themselves, lay 2 lemon slices on top of each fish, and then wrap each with 2 slices of bacon holding the lemons in place.

Heat a large cast-iron skillet over medium-high heat and coat lightly with the remaining 1 tablespoon olive oil. Place the trout, lemon side up, in the pan and cook for 3 minutes. Transfer the pan to the oven and roast until the trout are just cooked, 20 to 25 minutes, flipping the fish halfway through the roasting to ensure that the bacon crisps.

Lamb Stew
with Sherry and Mushrooms

SERVES 6

3 tablespoons olive oil

4 slices center-cut bacon

2 pounds lamb stew meat, cut into
1- to 2-inch cubes

4 cups button mushrooms, quartered

4 large carrots, cut into chunks

2 small Vidalia or other sweet onions,
cut into chunks

5 cloves garlic, smashed and peeled

¼ cup all-purpose flour

1 quart low-sodium beef broth

½ cup dry sherry

3 bay leaves

Kosher salt

Freshly ground black pepper

1 cup heavy cream

3 tablespoons chopped fresh Italian parsley

3 tablespoons chopped fresh tarragon leaves

1 (10-ounce) bag petite frozen peas

Buttered noodles, for serving

This is my granddaughter Eleyce's favorite dinner (she's three!). It's an easy, delicious meal, and even if *your* grandchildren aren't impressed, your guests will be. I have had a zillion compliments on the recipe and it's well worth the time it takes to make it.

If you don't care for lamb, feel free to use beef or chicken or any protein you prefer, but adjust time accordingly. Keep in mind that chicken cooks more quickly than lamb.

COMBINE THE OLIVE OIL and bacon in a large pot over medium-high heat. Cook the bacon, turning occasionally, until just crisp. Drain on a paper towel–lined plate, then coarsely chop and set aside.

Add the lamb to the pot and brown on all sides, about 3 minutes per side. As the pieces brown, remove them from the pot with a slotted spoon and reserve on a separate plate.

Add the bacon, mushrooms, carrots, onions, and garlic to the pot and stir. Sprinkle in the flour and cook 1 minute. Add the lamb, beef broth, sherry, bay leaves, salt, and pepper. Cover the pot, but leave a vent for the steam to escape. Bring the mixture to a simmer and cook until the meat is tender and almost falling apart, about 2 hours.

Add the cream, parsley, tarragon, and peas. Simmer until the peas are tender, about 8 minutes more. Discard the bay leaves. Serve the stew over buttered noodles.

Perfect Prime Rib

SERVES 8

1 (5-pound) boneless rib eye roast, with a fat cap, tied by your butcher

1 teaspoon granulated garlic

1 teaspoon granulated onion

Kosher salt

Freshly ground black pepper

¼ cup extra-virgin olive oil

2 tablespoons Worcestershire sauce

Prime rib was a Sunday dinner staple when I was growing up. Now it's a holiday tradition in my home, and it's also often a weekday treat when I cook for my friends. It's that easy and oh so good.

To ensure that the roast is cooked perfectly, use your meat thermometer early and often, as all ovens are different. Start checking the temperature earlier rather than later so that you don't overcook the beef. And remember, the meat will keep cooking once it's removed from the oven.

AN HOUR BEFORE you are ready to cook the roast, remove it from the refrigerator and place on a large platter or rimmed baking sheet. Rub it all over with the granulated garlic and onion and season well with salt and pepper. Drizzle with the olive oil and Worcestershire sauce and rub that in as well, turning to coat the roast. Let sit at room temperature for an hour, rolling it around occasionally to make sure it picks up the seasonings.

Preheat the oven to 450°F. Put the roast in a roasting pan and roast for 30 to 40 minutes, until the fat on the top of the roast is well browned. Reduce the temperature to 350°F and roast until the internal temperature of the meat is 120°F (for medium rare), 30 to 40 minutes more. Remove from the oven and let rest on a cutting board for 30 minutes. The temperature will continue to go up another 10°F or so as it rests.

Untie the roast, discard the strings, and carve into slices.

"LESS IS MORE."
—LUDWIG MIES VAN DER ROHE

The Mighty Bison Meatballs

SERVES 6

1 small onion, cut into chunks

1 small red bell pepper, cut into chunks

2 small stalks celery, cut into chunks

5 cloves garlic, smashed and peeled

1 cup fresh Italian parsley leaves

1 tablespoon chili powder

1 tablespoon cumin

2 teaspoons paprika

3 tablespoons extra-virgin olive oil

1 (28-ounce) can diced fire-roasted tomatoes

1 (10-ounce) can diced tomatoes with green chilies (such as Ro-Tel)

½ cup prepared barbecue sauce (such as Bone Suckin' Sauce)

Chipotle hot sauce or just regular hot sauce, to taste

Kosher salt

1¾ pounds ground bison (also labeled as buffalo)

2 large eggs

1 cup breadcrumbs

½ cup grated Parmesan cheese

Bison is a lean alternative to ground beef. Cooking it in a slightly smoky, mildly spicy, and very flavorful sauce keeps it from drying out. To keep prep work easy, I make the meatballs large (less rolling!), and for a healthier dish, I drop them right into the sauce to cook instead of frying them.

Serve the meatballs and sauce with pasta or any hearty grain, or a big chunk of corn bread for dipping. If bison is hard to find or you prefer beef, just use that.

IN A FOOD PROCESSOR, combine the onion, bell pepper, celery, garlic, and parsley and process to make a chunky paste. Scrape about one-third of the paste into a large bowl and set aside. In a small bowl, stir together the chili powder, cumin, and paprika.

To make the sauce, heat the olive oil over medium-high heat in a large Dutch oven. When the oil is hot, add the remaining vegetable paste. Cook and stir until it dries out, about 4 minutes. Add about two-thirds of the spice mixture and stir to combine. Add both kinds of tomatoes, the barbecue sauce, and hot sauce to taste, along with 1½ cups water. Season with salt. Let the sauce simmer while you form the meatballs.

For the meatballs, add the bison, eggs, breadcrumbs, Parmesan, and remaining spice mixture to the large bowl with the vegetable paste. Season with salt and mix with your hands just to combine; don't overmix. Form into 12 large meatballs, each about the size of a round lemon.

Gently drop the meatballs into the sauce, so they are all submerged. Simmer, partially covered and stirring occasionally, until the meatballs are cooked through and the sauce is flavorful, about 25 minutes. Let the meatballs sit in the sauce, off the heat, for 10 to 15 minutes before serving.

Tavern Ham

SERVES 10 OR MORE

....

1 (6- to 7-pound) fully cooked
boneless smoked ham

¼ cup orange marmalade

¼ cup grainy deli mustard

¼ cup packed light brown sugar

2 tablespoons cider vinegar

1 teaspoon ground ginger

¼ teaspoon ground cloves

....

This is a great buffet item. When the whole family is in town I make a 14-pound ham and serve it with cheesy scalloped potatoes or potatoes au gratin (same thing, different methods!). The ham is good served hot, at room temperature, or cold.

Cook the ham for about 20 minutes per pound: If your ham is larger or smaller than the 6- or 7-pounder used here, adjust the cooking time accordingly.

PREHEAT THE OVEN to 350°F. Cut off any tough skin from the ham and trim the fat to an even ¼ inch or so. Score the fat of the ham, but not down to the flesh, in a crisscross pattern all over. Set the ham, flat side down, on a rack in a roasting pan. Add 1 cup water and cover the pan with foil. Roast for 1 hour and 10 minutes.

In a bowl, stir together the marmalade, mustard, brown sugar, vinegar, ginger, and cloves. Brush the ham with some of the glaze. Continue to roast, brushing all over with the glaze every 15 minutes, until the ham is browned and crispy all over and the internal temperature reads 140°F, about 1 hour and 10 minutes more. Turn the ham on its side after 45 minutes of glazing and add more water to the pan if it looks like it's dried up and burning. Let rest 15 minutes before slicing.

Spring Chicken

SERVES 6

....

4 tablespoons unsalted butter

1 tablespoon dry mustard

2 teaspoons sweet paprika

1 teaspoon granulated garlic

½ cup honey Dijon mustard

½ cup cider vinegar

½ cup ketchup

½ cup lightly packed brown sugar

Hot sauce to taste

2 pounds boneless, skinless chicken thighs

Kosher salt

Vegetable oil, for the grill grates

....

This recipe's name has a double meaning. First, I like to think of myself as a spring chicken! (Although I can almost hear my son saying, "Not so much, Mom!") And second, it's spring and a great time to get the grill ready!

I use chicken thighs, but you can use any part of the bird.

MELT THE BUTTER in a small saucepan over medium heat. Add the dry mustard, paprika, and granulated garlic and stir to make a paste. Add the honey mustard, vinegar, ketchup, brown sugar, and some hot sauce. Cook just until the sugar dissolves and then whisk everything together to make a smooth sauce. Pour the sauce into a bowl and let cool completely.

In a large bowl, season the chicken lightly with salt and toss it with about 1 cup of the sauce. Let it marinate in the refrigerator for 1 hour, or up to 4 hours.

Preheat a grill to medium and brush the grates with oil. Transfer half of the remaining sauce to a serving bowl and set aside.

Grill the chicken, turning occasionally, until cooked through, 12 to 14 minutes, brushing the chicken with the remaining sauce, beginning when you first turn the chicken. Serve the chicken with the remaining bowl of untouched sauce for dipping.

Sausage Stew

SERVES 4

RICE

1 cup basmati rice

2 tablespoons unsalted butter

2 cloves garlic, chopped

½ teaspoon kosher salt

¼ cup chopped fresh Italian parsley

STEW

3 tablespoons extra-virgin olive oil

4 sweet Italian sausages (about 1 pound)

4 hot Italian sausages (about 1 pound)

2 medium onions, thickly sliced

3 Golden Delicious apples, cored and cut into 1-inch-thick wedges (you can leave the peel on or off)

1 tablespoon chopped fresh thyme

1 teaspoon paprika

2 tablespoons Calvados or regular brandy

1½ cups low-sodium chicken broth

1 bay leaf

Kosher salt

Freshly ground black pepper

1 tablespoon unsalted butter

Cider vinegar, to taste

My husband David always orders the sausage casserole when we go to Four Brothers Pizza in Valatie, New York. Knowing it's his favorite, I concocted my own, slightly altered, version: David fell in love with the nutty, slightly sweet-and-salty flavor combination of basmati rice, apples, and sausage.

The stew retains heat and travels well, making it a great dish to take to a party or potluck.

FOR THE RICE, rinse the rice in several changes of water in a strainer and drain it well. Melt the butter over medium heat in a medium saucepan. When the butter is melted, add the rice and garlic and stir to combine. Cook, stirring constantly, for 2 to 3 minutes, until the rice dries out a little, but don't let it brown. Add 1½ cups water and the salt. Bring to a boil, adjust the heat so the water is just simmering, and cover the pot. Cook, without peeking, until the rice is tender and the liquid is absorbed, about 20 minutes. Remove the

pot from the heat and let stand, covered, for 5 minutes. Fluff with a fork. Stir in the parsley.

Meanwhile, for the stew, heat a medium Dutch oven over medium heat and add the olive oil. When the oil is hot, add the sausages and brown on all sides, about 5 minutes. Transfer to a plate.

Add the onions to the fat left in the pan. Cook and stir until lightly caramelized, about 10 minutes. Add the apples, thyme, and paprika. Toss and cook until the apples are a light golden color, 2 to 3 minutes. Pour in the Calvados, let it simmer a minute, then add the broth and bay leaf. Season everything with salt and pepper and nestle the sausages into the onions and apples. Cover and cook until the sausages are cooked through and the apples are tender, 10 to 12 minutes.

Uncover the skillet and increase the heat to high to boil down the cooking juices to a thin glaze. Discard the bay leaf. Whisk in the butter and taste the sauce. Depending on your apples, it might be a little sweet. If so, drizzle in a teaspoon or two of vinegar. Give everything one more big stir and serve the stew over the basmati rice.

Rhubarb Hand Pies

MAKES 6 PIES

8 ounces rhubarb, cut into ¼-inch pieces

1 small Golden Delicious apple
(or other cooking apple), peeled and
cut into ¼-inch pieces

½ cup plus 2 tablespoons sugar

2 tablespoons unsalted butter

Juice of ½ lemon

1 tablespoon all-purpose flour
(plus more for rolling)

1 (14.1-ounce) box (2 crusts) rolled
pie crusts (such as from Pillsbury)

1 large egg, beaten with 1 tablespoon
milk or cream

¼ teaspoon freshly grated nutmeg

This spring treat is ideal for little hands and can be made with any seasonal fruit. And if your kids are picky eaters, this pie is a great way to introduce rhubarb, an early spring vegetable, into their lives. As soon as your children begin eating solid food, start giving them all the vegetables that are in season, and they'll know better than to turn up their nose if a delicious rhubarb pie crosses their path. Your likes and dislikes influence your child's eating habits. Think about it!

IN A MEDIUM SAUCEPAN, combine the rhubarb, apple, ½ cup of the sugar, the butter, and lemon juice. Bring to a simmer and cook until the rhubarb begins to break down and the apples have softened, 6 to 7 minutes. The filling should be somewhat thick at this point. Whisk in the flour, bring to a boil for a few seconds, and then scrape the filling into a bowl and let cool completely.

Preheat the oven to 400°F. On a lightly floured work surface, roll out the crusts to about a ⅛-inch thickness. Cut out 6 (6-inch) circles—a small plate works well as a template. Drop a dollop of the filling in the center of each round and brush the perimeter with the egg wash. Fold the rounds in half to seal in the filling, press out any air bubbles, and crimp decoratively. Put the filled hand pies on a parchment-lined baking sheet.

In a small bowl, combine the remaining 2 tablespoons sugar and the nutmeg. Brush the hand pies with some egg wash and sprinkle with the sugar mixture. Prick the top of each with a fork. Bake until golden on the top and bottom and the filling is bubbly, about 18 minutes. Cool on a wire rack and serve warm or at room temperature.

Raspberry Cheesecake

SERVES 8

CRUST

Nonstick cooking spray

6 graham cracker sheets

½ cup lightly toasted slivered almonds

2 tablespoons sugar

6 tablespoons unsalted butter, melted and cooled

FILLING

2 pounds cream cheese, softened

1 cup sugar

1 cup sour cream, at room temperature

6 large eggs, at room temperature

Grated zest of 1 lemon

1 teaspoon vanilla extract

½ teaspoon almond extract

TOPPING

½ cup seedless raspberry jam

2 tablespoons sugar

Juice of 1 lemon

2 half-pints raspberries

My ex-husband or, as I like to say, my *was-band*, never liked cheesecake. So when I made this for him, I fibbed and told him that he was eating vanilla pie with fresh fruit. For a silky smooth consistency, take the cream cheese out of the fridge at least an hour before you are ready to begin so it gets nice and soft. The almond flavors in the crust are a great natural pairing with raspberries.

This cake needs to chill in the fridge overnight, so it should be made a day in advance. Believe me, it's worth the wait, and everyone will love the wonderfully easy and very delicious cheesecake, ahem, I mean, *vanilla pie!*

FOR THE CRUST, preheat the oven to 350°F. Spray a 9-inch springform pan with cooking spray. In a food processor, combine the graham crackers, almonds, and sugar and pulse to make smooth crumbs. Pour the crumbs into a medium bowl and toss with the melted butter. Press the crumbs into the bottom of the prepared pan. Bake the crust on the middle rack until golden brown, about 15 minutes. Let the crust cool completely. Wrap the bottom of the pan, as well as the side (only about halfway), with foil. Set the pan in a roasting pan.

For the filling, reduce the oven temperature to 325°F. Bring a kettle of water to a boil. Beat the cream cheese in a mixer fitted with the paddle attachment on medium speed until light and completely smooth, 1 to 2 minutes. Add the sugar and sour cream and beat again until smooth and light. Add the eggs, one at a time, scraping down the bowl between additions. Beat in the lemon zest, vanilla, and almond extract. Beat just to combine. Pour the filling into the prepared crust in the roasting pan.

Set the roasting pan on the middle rack of the oven. Grab your kettle and add enough hot water to the

Continued

roasting pan to come halfway up the sides of the cheesecake pan. Bake until the edges of the cheesecake are completely set but the center still jiggles, about 1 hour and 15 minutes. Turn the oven off, leave the door slightly ajar, and let the cheesecake cool until just set in the center, about 30 minutes more.

Meanwhile, for the topping, combine the jam, sugar, and lemon juice in a medium saucepan. Bring to a simmer and cook until thick and syrupy, about 2 minutes. Add the raspberries and cook until heated through, but not falling apart at all, just a minute.

Scrape into a bowl to cool. Cover and refrigerate overnight.

Remove the cheesecake from the roasting pan and place on a rack to let cool completely. Cover and chill overnight in the refrigerator.

The next day, spread the cold raspberry topping over the cheesecake, cut into wedges, and serve.

Mocha Marvels

MAKES ABOUT 3 DOZEN

1 (12-ounce) bag semisweet chocolate chips

3 tablespoons unsalted butter

3 large eggs

1 cup sugar

1 tablespoon instant coffee granules

1 teaspoon vanilla extract

1¼ cups all-purpose flour

½ teaspoon baking powder

¼ teaspoon fine salt

Nothing is better than subtle notes of coffee in an afternoon treat. Coffee enhances and brings out the richness of chocolate, making the fudgy centers of these "marvels" a sinful pleasure. Perfect for an afternoon get-together with the ladies; they'll be begging you for the recipe before the day is over!

MELT THE CHOCOLATE chips and butter together in a double boiler or a bowl set over a pan of simmering water. Once melted, stir until smooth. Remove from the heat and let cool.

In a large bowl, whisk together the eggs, sugar, coffee granules, and vanilla. Whisk in the cooled chocolate mixture, then stir in the flour, baking powder, and salt. Put the bowl in the refrigerator for 30 minutes or so to let the batter thicken a bit.

Preheat the oven to 350°F. Make sure the rack is in the middle position. Line two baking sheets with parchment paper. Form the batter with heaping tablespoons on the prepared baking sheets, leaving an inch or two between cookies. Bake 10 minutes, or until the cookies are set around the edges but still fudgy in the center. Transfer to wire racks to cool. Repeat with the remaining batter until all of the cookies are baked.

*"LET FOOD BE THY MEDICINE,
AND MEDICINE BE THY FOOD."*
—HIPPOCRATES

Almond After-Dinner Bars

MAKES 12

¾ cup (1½ sticks) unsalted butter, softened

¾ cup sugar

1 large egg plus 1 large egg yolk

½ teaspoon almond extract

1½ cups all-purpose flour

¾ teaspoon baking powder

½ teaspoon fine salt

⅓ cup strawberry rhubarb jam
(or jam of your choice)

1 tablespoon amaretto

½ cup slivered almonds

These delightful bars are so versatile that you'll look for an excuse to make them. Dress them up or down: Place on an elegant dessert buffet and top with dollops of whipped cream, bring on a picnic in a brown paper bag, or just enjoy as an afternoon snack. I always decide how to serve the tasty treats based on what jewelry I'm wearing for the occasion!

LINE AN 8-inch-square baking pan with foil, with an overhang on two sides for gripping and removing the bars after baking.

In a mixer fitted with the paddle attachment, cream the butter and sugar on medium speed until fluffy, about 2 minutes. Add the egg, yolk, and almond extract and beat until smooth.

Add the flour, baking powder, and salt and mix on low just until the dough comes together. Flour your fingers and press about two-thirds of the dough into the prepared pan. Put the crust and remaining dough in the refrigerator to chill until firm, about 30 minutes.

Preheat the oven to 350°F. In a small bowl, stir together the jam and amaretto. Spread over the chilled crust, leaving a ½-inch border. Sprinkle the almonds over the top, then crumble the remaining dough over the almonds. Bake until the jam is bubbly and the topping is golden brown, about 35 minutes. Cool in the pan on a rack. Use the foil to lift the whole thing from the pan and cut into 12 squares.

The Chosen Chocolate Sauce

MAKES ABOUT 2 CUPS

4 ounces unsweetened chocolate (such as Baker's)

3 tablespoons unsalted butter

1¾ cups sugar

6 tablespoons corn syrup

1 tablespoon rum

Everybody loves a chocolate sauce—except my grandson Miles. He has never cared for chocolate. A saving grace, I suppose, for his parents and the dental bills! But my other 12 grandchildren love this sauce, as do the throngs of chocolate lovers I've served it to over the years! There are so many chocolate sauce recipes out there, and we've tried them all. This is our favorite, which is why we call it the "chosen" one.

This recipe will keep in a covered jar in the fridge for a week or two. If you'd like to warm it up for serving, do so gently in a heavy pan on low heat. It's great when drizzled over ice cream or a plain slice of pound cake. It also makes a nice dip for strawberries. Be creative, its uses are endless!

BRING ⅔ CUP water to a boil in a small pot. In a small heavy saucepan over medium-low heat, melt the chocolate and butter. Add the boiling water, then the sugar and corn syrup and bring to a boil. Keep the mixture at a slow boil for 8 minutes without stirring. Turn the heat down if the boil becomes too rapid. Remove from the heat and let cool. Stir in the rum. If you would rather not use rum, 2 teaspoons of vanilla extract is a fine replacement.

"ONE CANNOT THINK WELL, LOVE WELL, SLEEP WELL,
IF ONE HAS NOT DINED WELL."
—VIRGINIA WOOLF

Carrot Cake

SERVES 8 OR MORE

"'TIS AN ILL COOK THAT CANNOT LICK HIS OWN FINGER."
—WILLIAM SHAKESPEARE

CAKE

Softened unsalted butter and flour, for the cake pans

1½ cups granulated sugar

1 cup packed light brown sugar

1 cup vegetable oil

4 large eggs, lightly beaten

3 cups unbleached all-purpose flour (plus more for the cake pans)

1 (15-ounce) can pineapple rings, drained (reserve the liquid for the frosting) and chopped into ½-inch pieces

1½ cups shredded carrots

1½ cups shredded coconut

1 cup chopped walnuts, plus more for garnish if you like

3 tablespoons ground cinnamon

1 tablespoon almond extract

1 tablespoon baking powder

½ teaspoon kosher salt

FROSTING

8 ounces block cream cheese, softened

3 cups confectioners' sugar

4 tablespoons unsalted butter, softened

¼ cup pineapple juice from the canned pineapple

This recipe has served us well over many years. It's an excellent choice and it's always a crowd-pleaser—almost everyone I know loves carrot cake. You simply put all the ingredients in a bowl, mix it all up, put it in the pans, and set the timer! There has been many a birthday request for this cake. And many a dessert choice!

FOR THE CAKE, preheat the oven to 350°F. Make sure the rack is in the middle position. Grease two 9-inch round cake pans with butter and lightly flour them, tapping out the excess. In a large bowl, whisk together the granulated sugar, brown sugar, oil, and eggs. Add the flour, pineapple, carrots, coconut, walnuts, cinnamon, almond extract, baking powder, and salt and fold the ingredients together.

Divide the batter between the prepared pans. Bake until a toothpick inserted into each center comes out clean, about 40 minutes. Place the cakes on a cooling rack and let cool completely, then remove from the pans.

For the frosting, combine the cream cheese, confectioners' sugar, butter, and pineapple juice in a medium bowl. Mix on medium speed until light and smooth, 1 to 2 minutes.

To frost the cake, place one layer on a cake plate. Frost the top. Place the second layer on top. Frost the top, then the sides. Garnish with additional walnuts if you wish.

SUMMER

Chapter 2

SUMMER RECIPES

When summer arrives

When summer arrives on the farm, tiny seeds germinate in the warm soil and tomatoes, peppers, and corn begin to sprout. By the Fourth of July, the asparagus has gone to seed, the strawberries are ripe for picking, and the corn crops are knee-high in the cornfield. When I was growing up, my parents would warn me to keep out of our cornfield during the summer; a kid could easily get lost and not be able to find her way out!

Every June, I looked forward to when Grammy Carl and I would stroll down the dirt road alongside her house, scouring the hedgerows for early blackberries. Then we'd hurry home to make blackberry jam! I also looked forward to learning how to drive our Jeep truck so I could ride out to where my father, a dairy farmer, was baling hay under the beating summer sun. Knowing how to drive meant I could bring him some crisp iced tea or a freshly baked cookie. On days when rain was headed our way, the farmhands and my dad wouldn't stop for lunch because they had to get the hay off the field before the clouds rolled in. So I'd bring them ham salad sandwiches made from our own pigs or BLTs with fresh tomatoes from our garden.

Summer is a great time to make fruit pies and cobblers with your family for your July Fourth celebration, or just for some fun on a lazy summer afternoon! When I was raising my own kids on the farm, we'd go blueberry and raspberry picking in the summer and then head back to the house to make pies for dessert. And I'd serve them with homemade cinnamon whipped cream, of course.

Summer also offers you the lovely opportunity to prepare for the cold winter months. I always make my fruitcake in June and then cure it over the fall to serve at Christmastime. I keep the fruitcake moist with liquor and wrapped in plastic and foil in the refrigerator. I take it out every few weeks and pour a bit more liquor over it, repeating that process until Christmas. (My very best fruitcake is when I cure it every month for two years!) And every summer, I shuck, blanch, and freeze fresh corn so I can make steaming pots of corn chowder on cold December afternoons (you'll find the recipe for that on page 222).

These summer recipes are fresh, easy, and perfect for cookouts with your friends, summer evenings with your family, and any time your kids or grandkids come to visit!

"YOU CAN'T JUST EAT GOOD FOOD; YOU'VE GOT TO TALK
ABOUT IT TOO. AND YOU'VE GOT TO TALK ABOUT IT TO
SOMEBODY WHO UNDERSTANDS THAT KIND OF FOOD."
—KURT VONNEGUT

Polka-Dot Eggs

SERVES 1

2 large eggs

¼ cup shredded Cheddar cheese

¼ cup cooked broccoli florets

Pinch salt

1 teaspoon unsalted butter

This dish is particularly good for young kids. Using leftover or steamed broccoli, you'll cut the florets off the stalk so they fall apart and create polka dots when mixed with the eggs. The kids will never know they're eating broccoli! Just tell them that they're eating polka dots.

My grandchildren know that when they come to Gigi's home (they call me Gigi), breakfast is always scrambled eggs. Recently, my granddaughter Sydney said that she didn't like eggs and I replied, "Well, we're having Polka-Dot Eggs for breakfast, so perhaps you'll have a taste?" That taste turned into seconds!

WHISK THE EGGS, cheese, broccoli, and salt in a small bowl. Melt the butter in a skillet over medium heat. Add the egg mixture and cook, stirring, until desired consistency. Simply serve with buttered toast.

The Dashing Dog

SERVES 4

---

4 good-quality grass-fed all-beef hot dogs (from a butcher)

4 hearty hog dog buns (I use potato buns)

2 tablespoons unsalted butter, softened

Suggested toppings:

Warm sauerkraut

Spicy mustard

Ketchup

Banana pepper rings

Sliced jalapeños

A grilled hot dog is the epitome of summer. A simple get-together calls for a simple menu, and when you invite parents, grandparents, aunts, uncles, kids, and friends over, hot dogs are just the ticket. I use all-beef dogs because they're healthier. Add some potato chips and you're done!

And for dessert, don't forget the roasted marshmallows. If you're doing more than four dogs, a cast-iron griddle that goes over two burners is ideal, so you can grill them all at once.

PREHEAT A LARGE cast-iron skillet or griddle over medium heat. Split the hot dogs lengthwise. Smear the cut sides of the hot dog buns with a light coat of butter.

When the skillet is hot, set the buns cut side down in the skillet and press each one lightly to flatten a little. Toast lightly, about 2 minutes, then flip and toast the other side, just a minute. Remove to a platter.

Increase the heat to medium high, set the hot dogs cut side down in the skillet, and set another skillet on top to flatten them. Cook until well browned, 1 to 2 minutes, then flip and cook until the skin is crispy, about 1 minute. Serve the dogs, splayed open in the buns, with the toppings of your choice.

"I THINK PREPARING FOOD AND FEEDING PEOPLE BRINGS NOURISHMENT NOT ONLY TO OUR BODIES BUT TO OUR SPIRITS. FEEDING PEOPLE IS A WAY OF LOVING THEM."
—SHAUNA NIEQUIST

Picnic Pork and Pesto Salad

SERVES 4

1 (1½-pound) boneless pork loin roast, trimmed and tied

Kosher salt

Freshly ground black pepper

2 tablespoons extra-virgin olive oil

5 tablespoons basil pesto, store-bought or homemade

Juice of 1 lemon

¼ cup mayonnaise

¼ cup buttermilk

2 heads Boston or Bibb lettuce, torn, washed, and spun dry

6 slices bacon, cooked and crumbled

1 ripe avocado, halved, seeded, and diced

1 cup roasted jarred (or fresh, grilled) red bell peppers, chopped

We cooked a lot of pork on the farm when I was a kid. On hot summer days we'd serve this on the picnic table in the backyard. Then we'd wait an hour before taking a dip in the pond to cool off!

This is a wonderful summer lunch salad for any outdoor meal—all of the components can be prepped ahead of time, so you just assemble and dress the salad when you're ready to serve. The pork loin can be roasted and chilled up to a day ahead, but slice just before serving so it stays moist. This is not a big piece of meat, so don't overcook it or it will be dry.

PREHEAT THE OVEN to 400°F. Season the pork with salt and pepper. Heat a large oven-safe skillet over medium-high heat and add the olive oil. When the oil is hot, add the pork and brown on all sides, about 8 minutes. Brush the pork with 3 tablespoons of the pesto. Transfer the skillet to the oven and roast until the center of the pork registers 145°F on an instant-read thermometer, about 30 minutes. Let cool completely, then remove the strings and wrap the pork in foil. Chill overnight or until cold, at least 2 hours.

When you are ready to assemble the salad, whisk together the remaining 2 tablespoons pesto, the lemon juice, mayonnaise, and buttermilk in a medium bowl to make a dressing thin enough to drizzle (add a little cold water if needed).

Thinly slice the pork. Spread the lettuce on a large platter. Top with the sliced pork, then sprinkle with the bacon, diced avocado, and roasted peppers. Drizzle the dressing over everything, season with salt and pepper, and serve.

Turkey in a Tomato

SERVES 4

⅓ cup mayonnaise

2 tablespoons sour cream

1 teaspoon Dijon mustard

½ teaspoon granulated garlic

¼ teaspoon granulated onion

⅓ cup chopped fresh herbs (a combination of basil, parsley, and chives is nice, or use just one or two)

12 ounces chopped leftover Maple Syrup–Mustard Glazed Turkey Breast (page 31) or chicken

½ cup finely chopped celery

½ cup cooked fresh corn kernels

½ cup finely chopped red bell pepper

4 very large beefsteak tomatoes or other perfectly ripe summer tomatoes

Kosher salt

Freshly ground black pepper

Leaf lettuce, for serving

My first job was waitressing at my uncle Tom's restaurant, called the Tom Thumb. He was my mom's younger brother and he was like an older brother to me. I was 14 at the time, and I noticed that every old lady who entered the restaurant ordered this turkey salad in a tomato. Back then, every woman over 30 looked like an old lady to me, but they were all younger than I am today!

IN A LARGE BOWL, stir together the mayonnaise, sour cream, mustard, granulated garlic, and granulated onion. Stir in the herbs. Add the turkey, celery, corn, and red pepper. Toss to coat in the dressing, then refrigerate while you prepare the tomatoes.

Slice the very top from each tomato and reserve. With a spoon, scoop the center of each tomato into a strainer set over a bowl to collect the juices, leaving a hollowed-out tomato shell. Discard the seeds and pulp, but save the juices. Season the insides of the tomatoes with salt and pepper and let drain, upside down, on paper towels for 10 minutes.

When you are ready to serve, stir enough of the tomato juices into the turkey salad so it's moist but not wet, 2 to 3 tablespoons. Scoop the turkey salad into the hollowed-out tomatoes. Set the tops on at an angle and serve each tomato on a lettuce leaf or two.

Grammy Tabor's

Tuna Macaroni Salad

SERVES 6 OR MORE

1 pound mini penne, bow tie,
or elbow macaroni

1 cup mayonnaise, plus more as needed

¼ cup sour cream

¼ cup milk

2 (6-ounce) cans white tuna in water, drained

4 hard-boiled large eggs, chopped

2 stalks celery, chopped

1 medium onion, chopped

½ red bell pepper, chopped

¼ cup chopped fresh Italian parsley

1 tablespoon Dijon mustard

Juice of 1 lemon

1 tablespoon sugar

1 teaspoon granulated onion

1 teaspoon granulated garlic

Kosher salt

Freshly ground black pepper

My grammy Tabor, my mother's mother, was the salt of the earth. She prided herself on being the only person capable of disciplining me. She was a great cook and was always correct! I remember her making this old-fashioned salad for every single picnic or summer gathering we had—it was a summer staple. And now I make it for my grandchildren.

Tossing the pasta with a little milk is a great trick for pasta salads—it keeps the pasta from absorbing too much dressing. I use a whole box of pasta for this—it makes a lot. But you could easily cut it in half to serve three or four. Make the whole box and the salad can last a week in the refrigerator, but I bet it's gone in three days! It's that good.

BRING A LARGE pot of salted water to a boil. Add the pasta and cook according to package instructions until al dente. Drain the pasta well and transfer to a large bowl. Let cool slightly, then toss with the mayonnaise, sour cream, and milk.

Add the tuna, eggs, celery, onion, red bell pepper, parsley, mustard, lemon juice, sugar, granulated onion, and granulated garlic to the pasta and mix well. Season with salt and pepper. Add more mayonnaise as needed. And remember, taste as you go.

Kim's Brie Because It's Good

SERVES 4 TO 6

"TOMATOES AND OREGANO MAKE IT ITALIAN; WINE AND TARRAGON MAKE IT FRENCH. SOUR CREAM MAKES IT RUSSIAN; LEMON AND CINNAMON MAKE IT GREEK. SOY SAUCE MAKES IT CHINESE; GARLIC MAKES IT GOOD."
—ALICE MAY BROCK

1 (8-ounce) whole wheel of Brie

1 tablespoon extra-virgin olive oil (plus more for the baking dish)

3 cloves garlic, finely chopped

3 to 4 tablespoons honey

6 fresh sage leaves

Toasted baguette slices, for serving

Kim is my middle daughter and the one most likely to take home the award for best cooking! Kim is not a meat eater. She spent more time at the dining room table trying to finish her dinner than the dog spent under the table, sniffing for scraps! But she did love her garlic. So when she concocted this vegetarian appetizer, I knew it had to be excellent. And it is.

PREHEAT THE OVEN to 375°F. Select a ramekin or baking dish that is just large enough to hold the Brie, leaving about ½ inch of space around it. Brush the dish with olive oil. Put the Brie in the dish and drizzle with the olive oil. Sprinkle the garlic on top and drizzle with enough honey to cover the top. Arrange the sage leaves on top like the spokes of a wheel.

Bake the Brie until melted inside (if you press the Brie in the center, it will feel like a hot water bottle), 15 to 17 minutes. Let cool for 5 to 10 minutes, then serve with the baguette slices for dipping and spreading.

Melba Sauce
over Goat Cheese

SERVES 6 TO 8

1 (8-ounce) log goat cheese, softened

8 ounces block cream cheese, softened

1 tablespoon chopped fresh thyme

1 tablespoon extra-virgin olive oil
(plus more for the baking dish)

¼ cup chopped red onion

1 teaspoon ground cumin

½ teaspoon ground ginger

½ teaspoon yellow mustard seeds

Big pinch crushed red pepper flakes

2 cups chopped peeled fresh peaches

¼ cup chopped dried apricots or golden raisins

2 tablespoons raspberry vinegar

1 tablespoon light brown sugar

Kosher salt

Crackers or toasted baguette slices, for serving

The combination of peach and raspberry flavors is what makes this "melba," but you can use cider or red wine vinegar if you don't have raspberry vinegar. A little secret if you don't have a lot of time: Buy a jar of melba sauce, pour it onto a white plate, place a log of goat cheese on top, and sprinkle with coarse ground black pepper. But do this *only* if you haven't the time to do it properly!

PREHEAT THE OVEN to 400°F. Brush a 1-quart oval baking dish with olive oil. In a medium bowl, mix together the goat cheese, cream cheese, and half the thyme until smooth (or use a food processor). Spread the cheese mixture in the baking dish. Bake until golden on top and bubbly around the edges, 15 to 17 minutes.

Meanwhile, in a medium saucepan, heat the olive oil over medium heat. Add the remaining thyme, the onion, cumin, ginger, mustard seeds, and red pepper flakes and cook, stirring, until the onion is softened, about 4 minutes. Add the peaches, apricots, vinegar, brown sugar, and 2 tablespoons water. Season with salt. Simmer until thick and glossy, 5 to 6 minutes.

Spread the hot melba sauce over the goat cheese when it comes out of the oven and serve with crackers.

Basil Watermelon Bisque

SERVES 4 TO 6

6 cups cubed watermelon

Grated zest and juice of 2 limes

4 tablespoons extra-virgin olive oil

4 rings sliced pickled jalapeño
(plus some brine from the jar)

Kosher salt

Freshly ground black pepper

1 cup diced peeled cucumber

2 tablespoons chopped fresh basil

This soup is versatile and fun. The lime juice and pickled jalapeño add just the right amount of heat and kick, making it super refreshing on a hot summer day. I hold back on the jalapeño when I make it for my grandkids, but they are growing up so fast that it will be back in before I know it!

IN A BLENDER, combine the watermelon, lime zest, all but 2 teaspoons of the lime juice, 2 tablespoons of the olive oil, 3 of the pickled jalapeño rings, and a splash of the brine. Season with salt and pepper. Blend until very smooth. Taste and adjust the seasoning with a little more jalapeño brine, if needed, using up to 2 tablespoons total to balance the sweet and the spicy flavors. Transfer the soup to a bowl, cover, and refrigerate until completely chilled, about 3 hours.

When you're ready to serve, finely chop the remaining jalapeño ring and transfer to a medium bowl. Add the cucumber, basil, remaining 2 tablespoons olive oil, and remaining 2 teaspoons lime juice. Season the relish with salt and pepper and another splash of jalapeño brine.

Stir the chilled soup if it has separated. Then ladle into bowls and serve with the cucumber relish dolloped in the middle.

Potato-Leek
Such-a-Treat Soup

SERVES 6

4 tablespoons unsalted butter

6 medium leeks, white and very light green parts only, thinly sliced (about 2 cups)

2 medium russet potatoes (about 1½ pounds), cubed

1 quart low-sodium chicken broth

Kosher salt

Pinch freshly grated nutmeg

1 cup heavy cream

½ cup sour cream

1 to 2 tablespoons milk

Chopped fresh chives or dill, for garnish

This cold, creamy soup is a treat for those first hot days at the end of spring and the beginning of summer. It's easy as can be, but seemed daunting to me when I was younger. I was intimidated by it—probably because growing up on the farm, we ate hot soup only on cold days and it never occurred to me to make cold soup for hot days! When I married David many years later, I learned he loves cold soup, so I took the plunge and made this recipe. And now he requests it frequently.

If an unexpected chill hits, the soup is also good served hot.

MELT THE BUTTER in a large saucepan over medium heat. Add the leeks and cook, stirring often, until completely wilted but not browned, about 10 minutes (adjust the heat to keep them from browning if necessary).

Add the potatoes and stir to combine. Pour in the broth and season with some salt and the nutmeg. Bring to a simmer, cover, and cook until the potatoes and leeks are very tender, about 20 minutes. Stir in the heavy cream and remove from the heat.

Puree the soup in batches in a blender or right in the pot with a handheld immersion blender until completely smooth. Transfer to a bowl or large spouted measuring cup, cover, and refrigerate until completely chilled, about 2 hours.

To serve, stir together the sour cream and milk in a small bowl until smooth. If the soup has thickened too much, stir in a little milk, water, or cream to thin it to your liking. Serve the soup in chilled bowls, with a dollop of sour cream and a sprinkle of chives or dill.

Simply Simple
Spinach Soup

SERVES 4 TO 6

2 tablespoons unsalted butter

1 bunch scallions, chopped, reserving a handful for garnish

1 cup fresh shelled (or frozen) peas

1 quart low-sodium chicken broth

6 cups spinach leaves, tough stems trimmed

Pinch freshly grated nutmeg

Kosher salt

Freshly ground black pepper

½ cup chopped fresh Italian parsley

1 cup chilled plain Greek yogurt or sour cream, plus more for garnish

This is a great soup to serve with a pretty open-faced sandwich, such as a slice of rustic bread topped with basil pesto and sliced turkey. If you're using fresh (not frozen) peas, add 3 or 4 minutes to the cooking time, to cook just until the peas are tender. You can also serve the soup hot in colder months.

IN A LARGE saucepan, melt the butter over medium heat. Add the scallions and cook, stirring, until wilted but still bright green, about 2 minutes. Add the peas and chicken broth and bring to a simmer. Cook until the peas are tender, about 7 minutes. Add the spinach and season with nutmeg, salt, and pepper. Simmer just until the spinach wilts and is tender, about 4 minutes.

Transfer the soup to a blender or food processor (do in batches if necessary). Add the parsley and yogurt and process until smooth. Adjust the seasonings (salt and pepper to taste) and transfer to a bowl or pitcher. Refrigerate until very cold, at least 3 hours. Serve the soup in bowls, with a dollop of yogurt or sour cream and a sprinkle of chopped parsley.

Corn Relish and
Red Pepper Salad

SERVES 6

"THOUGH THEIR LIFE WAS MODEST,
THEY BELIEVED IN EATING WELL."
—JAMES JOYCE

4 tablespoons extra-virgin olive oil

2 cups corn cut from the cob
(about 2 ears)

1 small red bell pepper, chopped

1 small zucchini, chopped

1 teaspoon ground cumin

Kosher salt

1 (15-ounce) can black beans,
rinsed and drained

Juice of 2 limes

½ cup corn relish or corn salsa

1 avocado, halved, seeded, and diced

¼ cup chopped fresh cilantro

Hot sauce

Living on a farm meant we had fresh ingredients every day, and many days we had more fresh vegetables than we could consume! So we would wash Ball jars and set up the kitchen to get those fresh vegetables ready to preserve. That's how I learned to make corn relish!

If you have bacon left over from breakfast, you could take two crisp strips and crumble them over the salad just before you serve it.

HEAT A LARGE skillet over medium-high heat. Add 2 tablespoons of the olive oil. When the oil is hot, add the corn, bell pepper, zucchini, and cumin and season with salt. Toss and cook until the corn is just cooked, 3 to 4 minutes. Scrape everything into a large serving bowl and add the remaining 2 tablespoons olive oil, the black beans, lime juice, and relish. Toss well and let cool to room temperature (or refrigerate if making ahead).

When you're ready to serve, add the avocado, cilantro, and hot sauce to taste. Toss well and serve.

Simple Tomato Salad

SERVES 6

½ small red onion, thinly sliced

2 pounds assorted ripe tomatoes (big and small), cut into 1-inch chunks, or left whole or halved if tiny cherry tomatoes

1 English cucumber, diced

Kosher salt

Freshly ground black pepper

Generous pinch sugar

2 tablespoons red wine vinegar

¼ cup extra-virgin olive oil

1 cup crumbled feta cheese

¼ cup chopped fresh basil

I make this salad often. I run (not literally) down the road to Holmquest Farms, better known as Uncle Tom's, and grab a variety of tomatoes and run (not literally) right back home and toss the tomatoes into a bowl. In the height of summer, tomatoes need very little to dress them up—the basil and feta used here bring out their flavor perfectly. Serve the salad with some grilled chicken or seafood and that's dinner! Use whatever color and size tomatoes you can get your hands on. The more the merrier.

PUT THE RED onion in a small bowl with water and ice to cover and let soak 10 minutes to take away some of the bite of the onion. Drain and pat dry.

Put the onion in a large serving bowl with the tomatoes and cucumber and season with salt, pepper, and the sugar. Drizzle with the vinegar and olive oil and toss. Let sit for 5 to 10 minutes so the tomatoes give up some of their juices, then toss in the feta and basil and serve.

"TEACHING KIDS HOW TO FEED THEMSELVES AND HOW TO LIVE IN A COMMUNITY RESPONSIBLY IS THE CENTER OF EDUCATION."
—ALICE WATERS

Grilled Summer
Vegetable Kebabs

MAKES 8 KEBABS, SERVING 4 TO 8

2 medium bell peppers, cut into 1½-inch chunks

2 baby eggplants, cut into 1½-inch chunks

2 medium zucchini, cut into 1½-inch chunks

1 small red onion, quartered and layers separated (use the small interior layers for something else, as they won't fit on the skewers)

8 ounces halloumi cheese or other grilling cheese, cut into 1-inch cubes

½ cup extra-virgin olive oil

1 tablespoon chopped fresh thyme

1 teaspoon ground cumin

1 teaspoon paprika

1 teaspoon granulated garlic

Kosher salt

Freshly ground black pepper

This is a fun recipe to make with kids because they can help assemble the kebabs. Wash their little hands and don't let them play sword with the kebab sticks! Teach them how to gently handle the veggies so that when they're placing a vegetable on a skewer, they don't squeeze it too hard.

The cheese can be left out if you just want a straight veggie kebab, but halloumi is a nice, firm cheese that's easy to cut into cubes and holds up great on the grill. It's available in larger supermarkets, usually in the same place you find the feta. Or provolone will work—just order a thick slice at your deli counter.

PREHEAT THE GRILL to medium high. Soak 8 long wooden skewers in water for 15 minutes (or use metal skewers).

In a large bowl, combine the vegetables and halloumi with the olive oil, thyme, cumin, paprika, granulated garlic, and some salt and pepper. Toss well to coat everything with the oil. Thread the vegetables and cheese onto the skewers, alternating vegetables and cheese so they look pretty. Save any oil left in the bowl.

Grill the kebabs, turning on all sides, until the vegetables are charred in places and tender, about 12 minutes, brushing occasionally with the oil left in the bowl. Serve immediately.

Three-Layer Cheese
and Vegetable Terrine

SERVES 6 OR MORE

8 ounces block cream cheese, softened

1 (4-ounce) log goat cheese, softened

¾ cup (3 ounces) grated Parmesan cheese

2 small cloves garlic, finely chopped

8 tablespoons extra-virgin olive oil

Kosher salt

Freshly ground black pepper

2 cups loosely packed baby spinach

2 cups loosely packed fresh basil leaves

½ cup walnut pieces, toasted and coarsely chopped

½ cup chopped drained sun-dried tomatoes in oil

Crackers, for serving

I like to serve this simple and tasty spread at summer BBQs. It's great with crackers, as the recipe suggests, but I also like to use it as a dip for fresh vegetable crudités. One of my vegetarian friends even uses it as a schmear on her veggie burger!

IN A FOOD processor, combine the cream cheese, goat cheese, half of the Parmesan, half of the garlic, and 3 tablespoons of the olive oil. Process until smooth. Season with salt and pepper. Spread in the bottom of a 3-cup (or thereabouts) serving dish or bowl and spread so the top is flat.

Wipe out the processor and combine the remaining garlic, the spinach, basil, and ¼ cup of the walnuts. Process to make a chunky paste. Add the remaining 5 tablespoons olive oil and remaining Parmesan and process until smooth. Spread over the cheese layer.

In a small bowl, toss together the remaining ¼ cup walnuts and the sun-dried tomatoes. Spread over the green layer. Cover the bowl with plastic wrap and chill for at least 2 hours or overnight. Serve with crackers for spreading.

"It's Just Too Hot to Cook" Dinner

SERVES 4

8 slices sourdough bread

2 medium zucchini

1½ cups jarred roasted bell peppers, sliced

3 tablespoons balsamic vinegar plus 4 teaspoons for drizzling

6 tablespoons extra-virgin olive oil

½ cup fresh basil leaves

Kosher salt

Freshly ground black pepper

2 ripe summer tomatoes

1 (12-ounce) ball fresh unsalted mozzarella cheese

8 cups mixed baby greens

Crushed red pepper flakes (optional)

When David and I come home from work on a hot summer day and I don't want to cook, this recipe is a winner! It's a lovely, light dinner and the only heat you need to add is a few minutes of the toaster for the bread.

If you have a big family like my daughter Nita does, are throwing a simple dinner party, or are feeding a herd of hungry farmers, you might want to double the recipe!

LIGHTLY TOAST THE bread in the oven or a toaster and set aside.

Cut the ends from the zucchini. With a vegetable peeler, shave the zucchini, skin and all, into long ribbons into a large bowl, stopping when you get to the very seedy core. Add the roasted peppers to the bowl and sprinkle with the vinegar and olive oil. Tear the basil leaves into the bowl, leaving a handful for garnish at the end. Season with salt and pepper and toss well. Let sit while you assemble the rest of the ingredients.

Thickly slice the tomatoes and season with salt and pepper. Thickly slice the mozzarella.

Arrange the greens on 4 plates. Top with the toasts, then the sliced mozzarella, then the sliced tomatoes. Mound the marinated zucchini and pepper mixture on top of the cheese and drizzle the sandwiches with any dressing left in the bowl. Tear the remaining basil over the top and sprinkle with the red pepper flakes if you'd like a little heat. Drizzle with balsamic vinegar and serve immediately.

Summer Sunday Crab Cakes

MAKES 8 CRAB CAKES, SERVING 4

CRAB CAKES

1 pound lump crabmeat, picked over for shells

¾ cup unseasoned dry breadcrumbs, plus about 1 cup for dredging the crab cakes

½ cup mayonnaise

½ cup finely chopped red or yellow bell pepper

½ cup finely chopped celery (the inside leaves are nice in this too)

½ cup finely chopped red onion

1 large egg

Juice of ½ lemon

1 tablespoon Dijon mustard

1 teaspoon Worcestershire sauce

Kosher salt

Freshly ground black pepper

Vegetable oil, for sautéing

TARTAR SAUCE

¾ cup mayonnaise

2 tablespoons chopped fresh parsley or chives

2 tablespoons pickle relish

1 tablespoon Dijon mustard

Juice of ½ lemon

Dash of hot sauce

This recipe reminds me of my mother's cod cakes, which she made with dried cod. But I don't use dried cod out of the box like she did— they don't make it like that anymore! Today we call them crab cakes, yesterday we called them crab patties. My grandmother Tabor made many a patty, and you can as well. You can use salmon, cod, or any fish that might be left over from last night's dinner. You can also use surimi, sometimes labeled "krab," which is imitation crabmeat. You can always use canned salmon as well, which is a good staple to keep in your closet in case someone drops in or you're getting in late for dinner.

The quick tartar sauce is optional, but so easy to make and a nice accompaniment. You could also pair the crab cakes with cocktail sauce or a squeeze of lemon—or serve them on toasted buns with lettuce, tomato, and plain old mayo.

FOR THE CRAB cakes, in a large bowl, combine the crabmeat, ¾ cup breadcrumbs, the mayonnaise, bell pepper, celery, red onion, egg, lemon juice, mustard, and Worcestershire. Season with salt and pepper. Mix just to combine, don't overmix. If you have time, chill in the refrigerator for about 30 minutes to make it easier to form the crab cakes.

Spread about 1 cup more breadcrumbs on a plate. Form the crab mixture into 8 patties, just a little shy of 1 inch thick. Dredge the patties in the breadcrumbs on all sides and rest on a plate or baking sheet. Again, if you have time, let the crab cakes chill 15 to 20 minutes to firm up. (If you don't have time, that's fine too, just go ahead and cook them.)

For the tartar sauce, in a small bowl, stir together all the ingredients. Refrigerate while you cook the crab cakes.

Preheat the oven to 250°F and line a plate with paper towels. Heat about ½ inch vegetable oil in a large nonstick skillet over medium-high heat. The oil is ready when the tip of a crab cake sizzles on contact. In two batches, fry the crab cakes, turning once, until golden

Continued

brown on both sides and heated through, 6 to 7 minutes per batch. Drain the first batch on the paper towels and keep warm in the oven on a baking sheet while you fry the second batch. Serve immediately with the tartar sauce on the side.

My Son-in-Law's
Perfect Paella

SERVES 6

....

PAELLA

1 quart low-sodium chicken broth

1 teaspoon saffron threads

2 bay leaves

¼ cup extra-virgin olive oil

3 links (about 10 ounces) Spanish chorizo, cut into ½-inch rounds

1 pound boneless skinless chicken thighs, cut into 2-inch chunks

Kosher salt

Freshly ground black pepper

1 medium onion, chopped

1 red bell pepper, chopped

1 tablespoon tomato paste

3 cloves garlic, chopped

1½ teaspoons paprika (preferably smoked Spanish paprika)

2 cups paella rice (medium- or short-grain)

½ cup dry white wine

1½ cups frozen peas, thawed

1 dozen littleneck clams

1 pound large shrimp, peeled and deveined

¼ cup chopped fresh Italian parsley

2 lemons

1 loaf crusty country bread

SAUCE

1 clove garlic, chopped

1 cup mayonnaise

1 teaspoon lemon juice

½ teaspoon Spanish paprika

Pinch salt

....

Lazaro, my son-in-law, is quite an accomplished chef. An enthusiast who reads every cookbook he can get his hands on, he has made some of my favorite meals over the years. When he is in my kitchen, it's a real treat as he's not shy about helping out—or cooking an entire dinner for 30 people! I am blessed to have him.

This is one of his recipes—and one of my favorites. Depending on what protein you use, the flavors will vary. You can make this with any seafood (mussels, scallops, shrimp, or oysters) or any type of chicken and sausage (chicken breast, legs and wings; breakfast sausage or whatever your preference).

IN A SMALL saucepan, bring the broth, saffron threads, and bay leaves just to a simmer.

In a very large skillet or paella pan, heat the olive oil over medium heat. Add the chorizo and chicken and brown all over, about 5 minutes. Season with salt and pepper. Add the onion and bell pepper and cook until the onion begins to soften, about 5 minutes. Add the tomato paste, garlic, and paprika. Cook and stir until fragrant, about 1 minute. Add the rice, cooking and stirring to coat the grains in the oil, about 2 minutes. Add the wine and cook until reduced away, about 2 minutes. Add the hot broth, bring everything to a simmer, and tightly cover the pan. Cook until the liquid is mostly absorbed, about 12 minutes.

Continued

Quickly uncover and scatter in the peas and clams. Give everything a quick stir and cover the pan again. After 5 minutes, uncover and quickly add the shrimp. Cover and cook until the rice is done, the shrimp are cooked, and the clams have opened (discarding any that don't), about 10 minutes more. Let the pan rest off the heat for 5 minutes, then remove the bay leaves and stir in the parsley. In a separate bowl, combine the sauce ingredients. Squeeze the lemon over the paella and serve with the sauce and bread on the side.

Simply Grilled Swordfish
with Tarragon Butter

SERVES 4

½ cup (1 stick) unsalted butter, softened

2 tablespoons chopped fresh tarragon

2 tablespoons chopped fresh chives

2 tablespoons chopped fresh Italian parsley

Grated zest and juice of 1 lemon

1 clove garlic, finely chopped

Kosher salt

Freshly ground black pepper

4 (8-ounce) skinless swordfish steaks, about 1 inch thick

3 tablespoons extra-virgin olive oil

Fresh fish was not readily available on our farm unless someone went fishing in the pond or in the creek. Our good friend Tommy Mazur was our go-to fisherman and he always had the best catch! He even tried to teach our daughter Nita to fish, though I think it's the one and only time she touched a fish! Tommy is the be-all-end-all outdoorsman, which is hilarious because he married my not-so-outdoorsy best friend Lorinda. But just because she won't catch it doesn't mean she can't cook it! She learned how to grill swordfish with this amazing tarragon butter.

The recipe makes more butter than you'll need for the fish. You can halve the recipe if you really want to, but you'll find lots of other uses for the butter—on pork tenderloin, chicken, or other simple grilled fish or shellfish. And it freezes well!

IN A MEDIUM bowl, mix together the butter, tarragon, chives, parsley, lemon zest, and garlic. Season with salt and pepper. Transfer to a double thickness of plastic wrap, roll into a log, and chill in the refrigerator until firm, about 2 hours.

Preheat a grill to medium high. On a rimmed platter, drizzle the swordfish with the lemon juice and olive oil and season with salt and pepper. Let marinate at room temperature for as little as 10 minutes or up to half an hour.

Grill the swordfish, turning once, until just cooked through, 4 to 5 minutes per side. Top each piece of fish immediately with 2 thin slices of the tarragon butter and serve.

Everybody's Favorite
Lobster in a Roll

We never had lobsters on the farm—but four hours away, in Rockport, Maine, there were plenty! We would go for a weekend jaunt to Maine and on our way back stop at a local lobster house and load the cooler with lobster and seaweed. When we got home, we would boil the lobster for one meal and stuff ourselves with the tasty meat. The next day we'd make the most wonderful lobster rolls out of the leftovers. Here are the recipes for both.

BOILED LOBSTER

SERVES 2

Kosher salt for the water

2 (1½-pound) live lobsters

½ cup (1 stick) unsalted butter

Lemon wedges, for serving

FILL A LARGE stockpot with 8 quarts water and salt liberally (the water should taste like the sea). Bring to a rolling boil. Boil the lobsters for 13 minutes (begin timing when you put the lid back on).

While the lobsters are cooking, in a small saucepan, melt the butter over medium heat. Let simmer until the foam rises to the surface, 2 to 3 minutes. Let sit a minute or two, then spoon off the foam. Keep the clarified butter warm while you boil the lobsters.

Remove the lobsters with tongs and let rest for 5 minutes. Pour the clarified butter into serving ramekins, and serve with butter and lemon wedges.

LOBSTER ROLLS

SERVES 2

2 tablespoons mayonnaise

1 teaspoon lemon juice

1 teaspoon Dijon mustard

Big pinch granulated onion

¼ cup finely chopped celery (the lighter-colored inner leaves are good for this)

1 tablespoon chopped fresh chives

1 tablespoon chopped fresh parsley

2 cups cooked lobster meat chunks

Kosher salt

Freshly ground black pepper

2 potato or brioche hot dog buns

Melted unsalted butter, for brushing the buns

Lemon wedges, for serving

IN A MEDIUM bowl, combine the mayonnaise, lemon juice, Dijon, and granulated onion and mix until smooth. Stir in the celery, chives, and parsley, then fold in the lobster meat just to coat it in the dressing. Season with salt and pepper.

Heat a cast-iron pan over medium-low heat. Brush the cut sides of the buns with melted butter and toast in the pan, cut sides down, until golden, 2 to 3 minutes. Flip and toast the other sides, about a minute.

Stuff the rolls with the lobster salad and serve with lemon wedges.

Cold Grape and Chicken
Crunch Salad

SERVES 4 TO 6

CHICKEN

3 bone-in, skin-on chicken breasts
(about 2½ pounds total)

1 small onion, quartered

1 small carrot, cut into chunks

1 stalk celery, cut into chunks

1 bay leaf

2 sprigs fresh Italian parsley

2 sprigs fresh dill

2 teaspoons kosher salt

THE CRUNCH PART

½ cup mayonnaise

½ cup sour cream

1 tablespoon Dijon mustard

2 teaspoons honey

½ cup finely chopped red onion

¼ cup chopped fresh Italian parsley

2 tablespoons chopped fresh dill

Kosher salt

Freshly ground black pepper

1 cup halved green seedless grapes

1 cup halved red seedless grapes

2 stalks celery, chopped

½ cup coarsely chopped toasted walnuts

Whole Boston or Bibb lettuce
leaves, for serving

This recipe was a staple in my catering days. It's a lovely bridal brunch or ladies' luncheon dish, or an hors d'oeuvre on a crostini at a cocktail party (just mince the ingredients rather than chunk them). If you want to use leftover chicken in this recipe, you'll need about 3 cups. Don't throw out the liquid used to poach the chicken—it's a nice, light chicken stock that can be used as the base of a soup or stew. The chicken always has more flavor when cooked on the bone.

LEFTOVERS...

JUST ANOTHER DAY...

*JUST ANOTHER WAY...AND OFTEN
EVEN BETTER THAN YESTERDAY!*

FOR THE CHICKEN, poach the breasts earlier in the day, so they have time to cool: Put the chicken breasts, skin side up, in a pot just large enough to hold them and cover with cold water (about 2 quarts) by an inch. Add the onion, carrot, celery, bay leaf, parsley, dill, and salt. Bring to a simmer. Adjust the heat so the water is just barely simmering, cover, and cook until chicken is just cooked through, 12 to 13 minutes. Let the chicken cool in the poaching liquid.

Remove the chicken from the poaching liquid. Remove and discard the skin and bones and cut or tear the chicken into bite-size pieces; you should have about 3 cups.

For the crunch part, in a large bowl, stir together the mayonnaise, sour cream, mustard, honey, onion, parsley, and dill and season with salt and pepper to taste. Add the chicken, grapes, celery, and walnuts and toss to lightly coat in the dressing. Chill well, at least 2 hours, and serve in lettuce cups.

Boneless Breasts
with Boursin

SERVES 4

....

4 boneless, skinless chicken breasts
(about 2 pounds)

Kosher salt

Freshly ground black pepper

3 tablespoons extra-virgin olive oil

1 medium leek, white and light green part,
halved and sliced ½ inch thick

¼ cup dry white wine

1 cup low-sodium chicken broth

2 tablespoons unsalted butter

1 clove garlic, finely chopped

12 ounces fresh baby spinach,
tough stems trimmed

3 ounces herb and garlic soft cheese,
such as Boursin, softened

2 tablespoons chopped fresh Italian parsley

2 tablespoons chopped fresh tarragon

....

My daughter Abby loves this recipe for its fragrance and flavor. When they were growing up, I taught my children to never smell their food and Abby had such a hard time adhering to that rule when I made these aromatic chicken breasts.

Fresh tarragon works nicely in the sauce and gives it a somewhat unexpected flavor, but you could use all parsley if you want.

SEASON THE CHICKEN all over with salt and pepper. Heat a large skillet over medium-high heat and add 2 tablespoons of the olive oil. When the oil is hot, brown the chicken breasts on both sides, 2 to 3 minutes per side. Transfer to a plate.

Reduce the heat to medium and add the remaining 1 tablespoon olive oil to the skillet. Add the leek and cook, stirring, until softened, about 4 minutes. Add the wine and boil until it glazes the leek, about 2 minutes. Add the chicken and the broth, bring to a simmer, and cook, covered, until the chicken is cooked through, about 8 minutes.

Meanwhile, in another large skillet, melt the butter over medium heat. Add the garlic and cook until fragrant, about 1 minute. Add the spinach, toss to coat in the garlic butter, and season with salt and pepper. Cook until the spinach is wilted, 4 to 5 minutes.

Spoon the spinach onto serving plates. Put one breast on each portion of spinach. Add the cheese and herbs to the liquid in the pan and whisk until smooth. Spoon the sauce over the chicken and serve.

Burgers Burgers Burgers

Everybody loves a burger, so why not learn how to make them three different ways? For the beef burger, use chuck; it has more fat and therefore more flavor. Lamb has a high fatty content and luscious flavor, especially when mixed with goat cheese. But turkey, a recent trend, can be dry, so my turkey burger includes barbecue sauce and more condiments, which keep it flavorful.

BEEF BURGERS

MAKES 2 BURGERS

2 tablespoons mayonnaise

1 tablespoon ketchup

1 tablespoon pickle relish

1 tablespoon Dijon mustard

12 ounces ground chuck

2 tablespoons Worcestershire sauce

½ teaspoon granulated garlic

½ teaspoon granulated onion

Kosher salt

Freshly ground black pepper

2 ounces sharp yellow Cheddar cheese, cut into tiny cubes

2 onion rolls, split and toasted

Lettuce leaves, for serving

Sliced beefsteak tomato, for serving

PREHEAT A GRILL or grill pan to medium high. In a small bowl, stir together the mayonnaise, ketchup, relish, and mustard. Refrigerate the "special sauce" while you make the burgers.

In a large bowl, combine the ground chuck, 1 tablespoon of the Worcestershire, the granulated garlic, and granulated onion. Season with salt and pepper. Mix with your hands to combine. Sprinkle the cheese cubes over the meat and mix them in. Form into 2 (1-inch-thick) patties, tucking in any cheese cubes that stick out. Put the patties on a plate and season with salt and pepper and the remaining 1 tablespoon Worcestershire.

Grill the burgers, turning once, to your liking, or 8 to 10 minutes for medium. Serve on the onion rolls with lettuce, tomato, and the special sauce.

LAMB BURGERS

MAKES 2 BURGERS

3 tablespoons mayonnaise

1 tablespoon Dijon mustard

6 pitted Kalamata olives, chopped

4 tablespoons chopped fresh Italian parsley

12 ounces ground lamb

½ cup chopped scallions

2 cloves garlic, finely chopped

2 teaspoons ground cumin

1 teaspoon paprika (preferably smoked)

½ teaspoon granulated garlic

½ teaspoon granulated onion

¼ teaspoon allspice

Kosher salt

Freshly ground black pepper

2 (1-ounce) slices fresh goat cheese

2 ciabatta rolls, split and toasted

Lettuce leaves, for serving

Sliced beefsteak tomato, for serving

Sliced cucumber, for serving

PREHEAT A GRILL or grill pan to medium high. In a small bowl, stir together the mayonnaise, mustard, olives, and 1 tablespoon of the parsley. Refrigerate the olive mayo while you make the burgers.

In a large bowl, combine the lamb with the remaining 3 tablespoons chopped parsley, the scallions, garlic, cumin, paprika, granulated garlic, granulated onion, allspice, and some salt and pepper. Mix with your hands to incorporate the seasonings into the lamb. Form into 2 loose balls. Make a well in the center of each ball and stick the goat cheese inside, then pinch the lamb around to seal the goat cheese in and form a 1-inch-thick patty.

Grill the burgers, turning once, until done to your liking, or about 10 minutes for medium with melty goat cheese inside. Serve on the ciabatta rolls, with the olive mayo and lettuce, tomato, and cucumber.

TURKEY BURGERS

MAKES 2 BURGERS

....

¼ cup prepared barbecue sauce

1 tablespoon honey mustard

1 tablespoon peach or apricot preserves

12 ounces ground turkey (for juicier burgers, get regular ground turkey, not ground turkey breast)

¼ cup finely chopped scallions

¼ cup finely chopped red bell pepper

2 tablespoons dried breadcrumbs

2 teaspoons Cajun seasoning

Kosher salt

Freshly ground black pepper

2 thick slices pepper Jack cheese

2 potato rolls, split and toasted

Lettuce leaves, for serving

Sliced beefsteak tomato, for serving

Pickled jalapeño slices, for serving

....

PREHEAT A GRILL or grill pan to medium. In a small bowl, stir together the barbecue sauce, mustard, and preserves. Divide the sauce in half and refrigerate while you make the burgers.

In a large bowl, combine the turkey, scallions, red pepper, breadcrumbs, Cajun seasoning, and some salt and pepper. Mix with your hands to combine. Form into 2 (1-inch-thick) burgers. Season with salt and pepper.

Grill the burgers, turning once, for 5 minutes, until the exterior is cooked. Brush with some of the sauce then flip and brush the other side. Cook, turning once more, until the burgers are cooked through (turkey burgers need to be well done), 7 to 8 minutes more, adding the cheese on top during the last 2 minutes. Serve on the potato rolls with the remaining bowl of barbecue sauce, lettuce, tomato, and pickled jalapeños.

Grilled Flank Steak
in a Steakhouse Marinade
with Tomato Butter

SERVES 4 TO 6

STEAK AND MARINADE

1 (1-pound) flank steak, about 1 inch thick

1 teaspoon granulated onion

1 teaspoon granulated garlic

Kosher salt

Freshly ground black pepper

½ cup dry red wine

3 tablespoons Worcestershire sauce

3 tablespoons extra-virgin olive oil

TOMATO BUTTER

½ cup ripe cherry or grape tomatoes

½ cup (1 stick) unsalted butter, softened

1 tablespoon Dijon mustard

Kosher salt

Freshly ground black pepper

2 tablespoons chopped fresh chives

Flank steak was another staple on my farm and I have many recipes for it. This is just one of them that I made for my kids.

You'll have more tomato butter than you will probably use, but it keeps well in the fridge or freezer. It's good tossed with sautéed or grilled vegetables, white fish fillets, or shellfish. Remember to bring the meat to room temperature before you grill it.

TO MARINATE THE steak, season with the granulated onion and garlic, some salt, and lots of black pepper. Put the steak in a large resealable plastic bag and add the red wine, Worcestershire sauce, and olive oil. Seal the bag and marinate in the refrigerator for at least 4 hours or up to 8 hours.

For the tomato butter, preheat the broiler. Arrange the tomatoes on a baking sheet and broil until they pop and blister, 4 to 5 minutes. Let cool, then put in a food processor with the butter and mustard. Season with salt and pepper and pulse until almost smooth (a few chunks are okay). Add the chives and pulse just once or twice to combine. Scrape into a bowl and chill until solid, about 2 hours.

Preheat the grill to medium high. Remove the steak from the fridge when you turn on the grill. Remove the steak from the marinade and grill, turning once, until the internal temperature reaches 120°F for medium rare, 8 to 10 minutes. Spread 2 dollops of the tomato butter on top and let the steak rest 5 minutes. Slice the steak against the grain and arrange the slices on a platter with a few more dollops of the butter on top.

The Best of the Beef Stew

SERVES 6

All-purpose flour, for dredging

3 pounds beef or venison stew meat

Kosher salt

Freshly ground black pepper

¼ cup extra-virgin olive oil

2 large onions, thickly sliced

6 cloves garlic, sliced

1 cup dry red wine

1 (28-ounce) can Italian plum tomatoes, crushed by hand

2 cups low-sodium beef broth

1 teaspoon dried basil

1 teaspoon dried oregano

2 bay leaves

2 long strips lemon zest, removed with a vegetable peeler

2 long strips orange zest, removed with a vegetable peeler

¼ cup chopped fresh Italian parsley

This recipe is a chop-chop-in-the-pot. You can put dinner on the back burner of the stove, finish your chores, and then enjoy a delicious meal at the end of the day. This is a spin on an Italian-style stew, which I like to make with beef stew meat or venison stew meat from the leg or shoulder. My kids love it with mashed potatoes.

SPREAD THE FLOUR on a plate. Pat the meat dry and season with salt and pepper, then lightly dredge in the flour, tapping off the excess. Heat the olive oil in a large Dutch oven over medium-high heat. When the oil is hot, add the meat in batches and cook until browned, about 6 minutes per batch. Transfer the meat to a clean plate.

When all of the meat is out of the pot, reduce the heat to medium and add the onions. Cook and stir until the edges begin to brown, about 12 minutes. Add the garlic and cook until fragrant, about 1 minute. Pour in the wine and simmer until reduced by half, about 3 minutes. Add the tomatoes, beef broth, basil, oregano, bay leaves, lemon zest, orange zest, and 1 cup water. Bring to a simmer, return the beef to the pot, and cover. Cook at a bare simmer until the meat is tender, about 2 hours, uncovering for the last half hour.

Remove and discard the orange and lemon strips and the bay leaves. Bring the stew to a rapid simmer and cook until the sauce is reduced to your liking. Stir in the parsley and serve.

LIFE REVOLVES AROUND THE SKY FOR A FARMER.

RED SUN AT NIGHT IS A FARMER'S DELIGHT

RED SUN IN MORNING, FARMER TAKES WARNING

RING AROUND THE MOON AT NIGHT

SNOW OR RAIN SOON IN SIGHT.

Help with Hamburger

SERVES 4

2 tablespoons all-purpose flour

2 teaspoons chili powder

1 teaspoon paprika
(smoked paprika if you have it)

½ teaspoon dry mustard

½ teaspoon granulated garlic

½ teaspoon granulated onion

¼ teaspoon cayenne

1 tablespoon extra-virgin olive oil

1 pound ground beef

1 small onion, chopped

2 cups milk

¼ cup ketchup

2 cups uncooked elbow macaroni

2 cups (8 ounces) shredded yellow
Cheddar cheese

This meal was another staple on our farm. No matter which season we were in, we always had hamburger meat in the freezer. And when six hungry kids came through the door, I wanted to be ready to feed them! This cheesy one-skillet ground-beef dinner conjures up memories of the boxed mix we all grew up on, without all of the processed ingredients and preservatives. And it's very simple to prepare, which is necessary when life on the farm keeps you out working from dawn until dusk!

IN A SMALL bowl, stir together the flour, chili powder, paprika, dry mustard, granulated garlic, granulated onion, and cayenne.

In a large skillet, heat the olive oil over medium-high heat. When the oil is hot, add the ground beef and cook, breaking it up with a wooden spoon, until no longer pink, about 4 minutes. Pour off any excess fat from the pan. Add the chopped onion and cook, stirring occasionally, until softened, about 10 minutes.

Sprinkle the meat mixture with the seasoning mix and stir to coat the meat with the spices. Add the milk, ketchup, and 2 cups water. Bring to a simmer, add the macaroni, and cover. Simmer, stirring halfway through, until the pasta is al dente, about 10 minutes.

Add the Cheddar, stir just until it is melted, and serve.

*I'M A FARMER THROUGH AND THROUGH.
IT'S WHO I AM IT'S WHAT I DO.*

"WHERE THERE IS LOVE THERE IS LIFE."
—MAHATMA GANDHI

Chop-Chop-in-the-Pot
Cold Bean and Vegetable Soup

SERVES 6

2 cups vegetable tomato juice (such as V8)

¼ cup extra-virgin olive oil

1 tablespoon red wine vinegar

Kosher salt, to taste

¼ teaspoon cayenne pepper

1 large ripe beefsteak tomato, chopped (about 2 cups)

2 cups chopped unpeeled English or Persian cucumber

1 cup chopped celery

1 cup chopped bell pepper (red, yellow, or orange)

1 (15-ounce) can chickpeas, rinsed and drained

¼ cup chopped red onion

2 tablespoons chopped fresh Italian parsley

2 tablespoons chopped fresh chives

1 loaf crusty bread, for serving

1 wedge fresh cheese, for serving

This recipe is similar to gazpacho but easier to make because you leave everything chunky. The chickpeas make it hearty enough for dinner, especially if you serve it with a nice piece of cheese and a loaf of good bread to round out the meal.

The soup tastes best when you make it ahead of time and refrigerate it so that the vegetables give up their juices to make a flavorful, cold broth. It will look its best if you chop all the vegetables about the same size.

IN A LARGE serving bowl, whisk together the vegetable juice, olive oil, and vinegar. Season with salt and cayenne pepper. Add the tomato, cucumber, celery, pepper, and chickpeas and toss well. Add the onion to the bowl and toss. Cover and refrigerate until well chilled, at least 1 hour or up to 8 hours.

To serve, stir in the parsley and chives and spoon the soup into bowls, with hunks of crusty bread for dipping and cheese for spreading on the bread. This can also be eaten hot.

The Best Peanut Butter Cookies

MAKES 24 COOKIES

1 cup creamy peanut butter

¾ cup (1½ sticks) unsalted butter, softened

¼ cup vegetable shortening

1¾ cups packed light brown sugar

2 large eggs, at room temperature

1 tablespoon pure vanilla extract

2¾ cups all-purpose flour

1¼ teaspoons baking soda

¼ teaspoon kosher salt, plus more for sprinkling

1 cup peanut butter chips

Any flavor fruit jam

The inspiration for this recipe comes from my grammy Carl—she was the queen of homemade cookies. They are so good!

For a little something extra special, I put a dollop of jelly in the center after baking. While the cookies are still hot, I make an indentation the size of a thumbprint in the center of the cookie, which I fill with jam.

PREHEAT THE OVEN to 375°F. In the bowl of an electric mixer fitted with the paddle attachment, combine the peanut butter, butter, and shortening and beat on medium speed until light and smooth, about 2 minutes. Add the brown sugar and cream until light and fluffy, about 2 minutes. Add the eggs, one at a time, beating well in between each addition. Beat in the vanilla and combine until mixed.

Whisk the flour, baking soda, and salt together in a medium bowl. Add the flour in 3 additions to the peanut butter mixture, beating until just combined. Stir in the peanut butter chips.

Use a 2-ounce ice cream scoop and scoop balls of dough onto a baking sheet.

Bake the cookies on the middle oven rack on a greased baking sheet for 13 minutes. Transfer cookies to a rack to cool. Don't forget to make an indentation in your cookies for the jam. Repeat to bake the remaining cookies.

Any Fresh Fruit Cobbler

SERVES 6 TO 8

FILLING

½ cup sugar

1½ tablespoons cornstarch

¼ teaspoon ground cinnamon

4 cups (1-inch) chunked peaches or
other stone fruit (about 4 large peaches,
more for smaller fruits), peeling optional

1½ cups blueberries or other berries

Grated zest and juice of ½ lemon

TOPPING

1½ cups all-purpose flour

¼ cup sugar

1 teaspoon baking powder

½ teaspoon baking soda

¼ teaspoon fine salt

6 tablespoons cold unsalted butter,
cut into pieces

¾ cup buttermilk

This is another farmhouse staple. You can make the cobbler with any combination of summer stone fruits (peaches, apricots, nectarines, plums, even pitted cherries) and berries (blueberries, raspberries, blackberries), but I particularly like the combination of peaches and blueberries. For a more refined version, you can peel the peaches, but it's fine to leave the skins on. Serve warm with whipped cream or vanilla ice cream.

PREHEAT THE OVEN to 375°F. For the filling, whisk together the sugar, cornstarch, and cinnamon. Add the fruit, berries, and lemon zest and juice and toss together. Let sit while you make the topping.

For the topping, stir together the flour, sugar, baking powder, baking soda, and salt in a large bowl (a food processor does this very easily as well). Drop in the butter pieces and cut into small bits with a pastry blender or 2 knives. Drizzle in the buttermilk and toss with a fork just until a sticky dough comes together.

Pour the fruit filling into an 8-inch-square baking dish. Drop the topping by spoonfuls onto the filling, covering the top. Bake until the topping is golden and set and the filling is bubbling all over, 35 to 40 minutes. Let cool on a rack at least 30 minutes before serving.

Just Simple
Strawberry Shortcake
with a Secret

SERVES 6

STRAWBERRIES

1 quart strawberries (1 pound), stemmed, hulled, and halved or quartered, depending on size

3 tablespoons strawberry jam

BISCUITS

2 cups all-purpose flour

1 tablespoon sugar, plus more for sprinkling the biscuits

1 tablespoon baking powder

¼ teaspoon fine salt

1 to 1¼ cups heavy cream, plus more for brushing the biscuits

WHIPPED CREAM

1 cup heavy cream

1 tablespoon sugar

¼ teaspoon vanilla extract

3 to 4 tablespoons unsalted butter, softened, for buttering the biscuits

The secret to this recipe is to bake the biscuits just before serving them. As soon as they come out of the oven, split them and butter them right away. And don't dillydally when making the whipped cream. There is nothing better than warm strawberry shortcake with cold whipped cream! Another little tip: I add a small amount of strawberry jam to the strawberries if they need to be sweetened. It enhances the flavor.

FOR THE STRAWBERRIES, in a large bowl, toss the strawberries and jam together and let sit while you make the biscuits.

For the biscuits, preheat the oven to 425°F and line a baking sheet with parchment. Sift together the flour, sugar, baking powder, and salt in a large bowl. Pour in 1 cup cream and stir quickly to make a shaggy dough (mixed enough to incorporate the ingredients but still with visible lumps). Add up to another ¼ cup cream, if needed, to bring the dough together. Dump the dough onto a floured counter, knead a couple of times, and pat gently until it is slightly thicker than ½ inch. Use a 2-inch round cutter to cut out 12 rounds. Put the rounds, spaced so they aren't touching, on the prepared baking sheet. Brush the tops with a little cream and sprinkle with a little sugar. Bake until puffed and light golden on the edges, 13 to 14 minutes.

While the biscuits bake, whip the cream: Beat in a medium bowl until frothy with a whisk or handheld mixer. Add the sugar and vanilla and whisk until the cream forms soft peaks.

To serve, split and butter the warm biscuits. Put the bottoms of 2 biscuits on each of 6 plates. Spoon some strawberries and whipped cream over each and top with the biscuit tops. Finish with more whipped cream and any remaining strawberries.

Simply Syrupy
Sections of Fruit

SERVES 6

6 tablespoons sugar

2 tablespoons Chambord (raspberry liqueur) or other berry liqueur

1 quart strawberries (1 pound)

½ cup blueberries

½ cup blackberries

1 cup peaches

1 cup cold heavy cream

½ teaspoon ground cinnamon

Crisp cookies, like tuiles or shortbread, for serving

I would be lost without Farmer Fred! On my farm in Copake, New York, he has worked the fields, cared for the cows, and provided me with all the milk and cream I need for the last 30 years. He is my hero and without him I don't know how I would adorn my delicious desserts. Where else would I get ice cream made with such love and care? Thank you, Farmer Fred!

IN A SMALL saucepan, combine 4 tablespoons of the sugar with ¼ cup water. Bring to a simmer to dissolve the sugar. Cool and stir in the Chambord, to taste.

Hull the strawberries and halve them if small or quarter them if large. Toss them with the blueberries, blackberries, peaches, and cooled syrup and refrigerate until chilled, about 2 hours.

When you're ready to serve, whisk the cold cream in a large bowl until foamy. Sprinkle in the remaining 2 tablespoons sugar and the cinnamon and whisk until soft peaks form.

To serve, spoon the fruit and syrup into serving glasses. Dollop the whipped cream on top and serve each with a cookie alongside.

*"FOOD IS SYMBOLIC OF LOVE
WHEN WORDS ARE INADEQUATE."*
—ALAN D. WOLFELT

Silly Sweet Squares

MAKES 16 PIECES

CRUST

1¼ cups all-purpose flour

6 tablespoons confectioners' sugar

½ teaspoon salt

6 tablespoons cold unsalted butter, cut into pieces (plus more butter for the baking pan)

1 large egg, beaten with 1 tablespoon cold water

TOPPING

½ cup honey

¼ cup light brown sugar

2 tablespoons heavy cream

Pinch kosher salt

4 tablespoons cold unsalted butter, cut into pieces

½ teaspoon vanilla extract

2 cups very coarsely chopped toasted unsalted nuts

This is a simple recipe that satisfies the desire for something sweet after a savory dinner. I call them Silly Sweet Squares because my silly grand-daughter Bailey just gobbles them up, and of course the sugar just makes her sillier!

Make sure the nuts are just barely chopped, so they don't get pasty when you stir them into the sugar syrup.

FOR THE CRUST, preheat the oven to 350°F. Line an 8-inch-square baking pan with foil, with an overhang on both sides for gripping and removing the bars after baking. Butter the foil and fit a square of parchment paper on the bottom or just grease the pan.

In a food processor, combine the flour, confectioners' sugar, and salt. Pulse to combine. Add the butter pieces and pulse until the mixture resembles a coarse meal. Sprinkle in the egg mixture and pulse just until the dough comes together. The dough should be crumbly but not dry. If it's dry, add a teaspoon of water and pulse again.

Press the dough into the prepared pan to make an even crust on the bottom. Bake for 20 minutes. Cool the crust completely.

For the topping, combine the honey, brown sugar, cream, and salt in a medium saucepan. Bring to a simmer and cook until the sugar is dissolved, about 2 minutes. Add the butter and boil, stirring, until very smooth, about 3 minutes. Remove from the heat and stir in the vanilla and nuts. Pour over the crust. Let cool on a rack until the nuts are set, about 2 hours. Remove the bars by the foil handles and cut into 16 squares.

FALL

Chapter 3

FALL RECIPES

On the farm, fall is all about reaping the rewards of what was sown in the spring. It's the time to harvest the heartier fruits and vegetables that will sustain the family through the cold-weather months, such as acorn and Hubbard squash, pumpkin, and potatoes. I store them in the cellar during the winter and they keep well for months due to their thick skins and meaty flesh. One of my favorite things to do is to create a ratatouille, a traditional French stewed vegetable dish, and serve it with my Basic Bone-In Pork Roast (page 181) and creamed potatoes.

Apples are another seasonal favorite on the farm and farmhouse apple pies are a traditional fall dessert. When I was a child, I peeled apples with my grandmother to make fresh apple pie. I continued the tradition with my own children and now my grandkids love to do it too. Use my Just the BEST Apple Pie recipe (page 195) and put your kids to work as apple peelers. The pie will taste that much better to them if they've rolled up their sleeves and done some of the work. And don't forget to remind them that the child who peels the most apples gets the biggest piece of pie!

Oatmeal with Kisses

SERVES 4

1½ cups milk

1½ cups oatmeal

½ teaspoon salt

4 chocolate kisses

1 tablespoon brown sugar

Mini chocolate chips to sprinkle over the top (optional)

Last Christmas, the breakfast menu for my family of 26 included this special twist on hot oatmeal. It can be difficult to entice the grand-kids to eat oatmeal for breakfast, so I decided to place a Hershey's chocolate kiss at the bottom of each bowl. They loved it, and so did their parents! Don't forget to unwrap the chocolate kiss.

HEAT THE MILK in a medium saucepan over medium heat until it simmers. Add the oatmeal and salt and bring to a boil. Turn down the heat, cover, and simmer for 5 minutes, or according to package directions. Unwrap the chocolate kisses and put at the bottoms of 4 bowls. Divide the oatmeal among the bowls and sprinkle with brown sugar and the optional mini chocolate chips (and call them *mini kisses*).

Simply Savory
Perfect Pear Tart

SERVES 4 TO 6

3 small or 2 large ripe Bosc pears, peeled, cored, and sliced ¼ inch thick

Juice of 1 lemon

3 tablespoons light brown sugar

1 tablespoon unsalted butter, cut into pieces

2 teaspoons cornstarch

1 teaspoon chopped fresh thyme

1 teaspoon chopped fresh sage

Kosher salt

Freshly ground black pepper

1 refrigerated rolled pie crust dough or 1 recipe Pie Dough (page 195)

3 ounces Stilton or other crumbly blue cheese, crumbled

1 large egg, beaten

This savory tart is a rustic fall delight and a wonderful lunch dish. It's more for the adult children in my life than the little ones! My daughter Sarah loves pears and she's the one I make this for the most.

The tart, with a side salad, will serve 4 for lunch or a light dinner. Cut it into 6 wedges if you're serving as an appetizer. If you'd like to make your own homemade pie dough, you may want to add a few minutes to the final cooking time, as purchased dough tends to brown more quickly than homemade.

PREHEAT THE OVEN to 425°F. In a large bowl, toss together the pears, lemon juice, brown sugar, butter, cornstarch, thyme, and sage. Season with a little salt and pepper, remembering that the Stilton is salty and has a bite to it.

On a piece of parchment paper, roll the pie dough into a rough 14-inch circle and use a pizza cutter to trim to a relatively neat circle. Slide onto a flat baking sheet (right on the parchment). Place half of the pear filling in the center, leaving a 2-inch border. Sprinkle the filling with half of the Stilton. Top with the remaining filling, then the remaining Stilton. Fold the crust up over the filling, overlapping to form a nice pattern. Bake on the bottom rack of the oven until the crust is just set, about 12 minutes. Brush with the beaten egg and bake until the filling is bubbly and the crust is golden brown, 15 to 18 minutes more. Cool on a rack for at least 20 minutes before serving warm or at room temperature.

Grampy Jim's
Ham Sandwich

MAKES 1 SANDWICH

2 teaspoons Dijon mustard

2 teaspoons mayonnaise

2 thick slices hearty white sandwich bread, from a bakery

1 tablespoon unsalted butter, softened (plus more for the skillet)

2 thin rings sliced red onion

2 ounces thinly sliced Gruyère cheese (about 2 slices)

2 to 3 ounces thinly sliced ham, from a good baked ham

¼ avocado, sliced

Kosher salt

Freshly ground black pepper

My dad, the old farmer that he was and a man of few words, would refer to someone he was not fond of (one of his granddaughters' boyfriends, usually) as being "useless as a ham sandwich." I have no idea where this expression came from, but this sandwich is not useless—it's delicious.

A well-seasoned cast-iron skillet or griddle makes the best toasted sandwich. I like to press down on the sandwich a little, over low heat, while cooking—not so much that I smush the sandwich, but just enough so that everything melts evenly and comes together in one nice package of flavors.

HEAT A CAST-IRON skillet over medium-low heat. In a small bowl, stir together the mustard and mayo. Lay the bread flat on your work surface and spread the top sides with the softened butter.

Brush the skillet with a film of butter and lay down one slice of bread, butter side down. Spread with half the mayo mustard, top with the red onion, half the cheese, all of the ham, the avocado, and season with salt and pepper. Top with the remaining cheese. Spread the remaining mayo mustard on the naked side of the last slice of bread and set on top of the cheese, butter side up.

Cook the sandwich, pressing down lightly with a metal spatula, until golden on the underside, adjusting the heat so this takes a good 4 to 5 minutes. Flip and brown the other side, pressing to toast the second side in the same way, until the sandwich is crisp and golden and the cheese is oozy and melting, another 4 to 5 minutes. Transfer to a cutting board, cut in half, and serve.

To-Fall-For
Sumptuous Salad

SERVES 4 TO 6

3 tablespoons cider vinegar

3 tablespoons sour cream

2 tablespoons grainy Dijon mustard

1 tablespoon pure maple syrup

3 tablespoons extra-virgin olive oil

2 tablespoons chopped fresh herbs
(parsley, chives, basil, chervil, dill, or
a combination of whatever you have)

Kosher salt

Freshly ground black pepper

1 bunch watercress, tough stems
trimmed (about 6 cups loosely packed)

6 cups loosely packed baby arugula

1 large red apple, halved, cored,
and sliced (Gala is a good choice)

2 Belgian endive, sliced crosswise
¼ inch thick

1½ cups seedless grapes

4 ounces blue cheese (such as
Maytag blue), crumbled

½ cup coarsely chopped toasted walnuts

4 ounces thinly sliced prosciutto

The flavors of fall are combined in this salad. The creamy dressing and prosciutto make it hearty enough for a main course with a hot loaf of bread served alongside it. If you can find speck, a lightly smoked Northern Italian version of prosciutto, it makes this a seasonal favorite.

IN A SPOUTED measuring cup, whisk together the vinegar, sour cream, mustard, and maple syrup. Drizzle in the olive oil while you whisk to make a smooth dressing. Stir in the herbs, season with salt and pepper, and refrigerate while you assemble the salad.

Spread the greens on a large platter. Top with the apple, endive, grapes, blue cheese, and walnuts. Drape and fold the prosciutto over the top. Drizzle all over with about two-thirds of the dressing. Serve the rest of the dressing in a bowl alongside at the table.

Root Vegetable One-Dish

SERVES 4

2 tablespoons unsalted butter
(plus more for the baking dish)

3 cloves garlic, chopped

3 cups heavy cream

2 bay leaves

1 small celery root (about 12 ounces),
peeled and thinly sliced

2 medium parsnips (about 10 ounces),
peeled and thinly sliced

1 pound sweet potatoes,
peeled and thinly sliced

1 medium rutabaga (about 12 ounces),
peeled and thinly sliced

1 pound Yukon gold potatoes, thinly sliced

2 tablespoons chopped fresh sage leaves

1 tablespoon chopped fresh thyme

Kosher salt

Freshly ground black pepper

8 ounces medium-sharp yellow
Cheddar cheese, grated

¾ cup (3 ounces) grated Parmesan cheese

This is one of my crowd-pleasers. I serve it with a large baked ham and spicy mustard. It's a perfect lunch with a loaf of bread or a side of pasta.

PREHEAT THE OVEN to 400°F. Butter a lasagna pan or other 4-quart baking dish. In a medium saucepan, melt the butter over medium heat. Add the garlic and cook until sizzling, about 1 minute, then pour in the cream and add the bay leaves. Bring to a simmer and remove from the heat.

Toss all of the vegetables with the sage and thyme in a large bowl and season well with salt and pepper. Layer half of the vegetables in the prepared dish. Sprinkle with half of both cheeses. Layer the remaining vegetables on top. Remove the bay leaves from the hot cream and pour the cream over the vegetables. Sprinkle with the remaining Cheddar and Parmesan. Place the dish on a baking sheet and cover with foil (tenting it, so it doesn't touch the cheese). Bake until the vegetables are just tender and the cream is bubbly, 1 to 1¼ hours. Remove the foil and continue to bake until golden on top, about 45 minutes more. Let rest 20 minutes before serving.

Autumn "Dates" Night Bread

MAKES 1 LOAF

1½ cups chopped pitted dates

2 cups all-purpose flour
(plus more for the pan)

2 teaspoons baking powder

½ teaspoon baking soda

2 teaspoons pumpkin pie spice

¼ teaspoon fine salt

6 tablespoons unsalted butter
(plus more for the pan)

¾ cup packed dark brown sugar

2 large eggs

½ cup sour cream

2 tablespoons dark rum or brandy

1 teaspoon vanilla extract

¼ cup milk

1 cup coarsely chopped
toasted walnuts

My kids, and their kids, love hors d'oeuvres—
and this recipe feeds them all! The thinner it's
sliced, the more people it feeds. The slices can
also be cut in half. The rule in my house is no
food outside the kitchen, but my granddaughter
Isabella loves this bread so much that she sneaks
it out by putting it in her pocket!

Serve the bread sliced with herbed Boursin or a
sharp Cheddar and some grapes. It will keep for
several days if well wrapped—if you don't have
a huge family that will gobble it all up in one
sitting! It is also a nice breakfast treat, toasted
with cream cheese.

PREHEAT THE OVEN to 350°F. Butter and flour an
8½- by 4½-inch loaf pan and line the bottom with
parchment paper. Bring ½ cup water to a boil in a small
saucepan. Add the dates and set aside until cool. Drain.

Sift together the flour, baking powder, baking soda,
pumpkin pie spice, and salt onto a piece of parchment
paper. Set aside.

In a mixer fitted with the paddle attachment, cream
the butter and brown sugar on high speed until fluffy,
about 2 minutes. Add the eggs and sour cream and
beat to combine, scraping the bowl down. Add the rum
and vanilla and beat to combine. Add the flour mixture
on low speed until just combined. Add the milk, increase
the speed to medium, and beat until just smooth, about
15 seconds. Add the drained dates and the nuts and stir
just until distributed.

Scrape the batter into the prepared pan. Bake until a
toothpick comes out clean, 50 to 60 minutes. Cool in
the pan on a rack for 15 minutes, then unmold and cool
completely before slicing.

Butternut Because Soup

SERVES 6 PLUS LEFTOVERS

2 tablespoons unsalted butter

4 slices bacon, chopped

2 medium leeks, white and light green parts, sliced (about 3 cups)

1 large fresh butternut squash, peeled, seeded, and cut into 1-inch chunks

2 teaspoons chopped fresh thyme

¼ teaspoon freshly grated nutmeg

Kosher salt

1½ quarts low-sodium chicken broth

1 large Golden Delicious apple, peeled, cored, and cut into 1-inch chunks

½ cup sour cream

1 to 2 tablespoons milk

By the time fall rolls around, I'm ready for butternut squash in everything! It's one of my favorite ingredients and gives food such a vibrant color.

I love using uncured applewood smoked bacon when I can find it, but if you want to make this vegetarian-friendly, leave out the bacon and simply substitute about 2 tablespoons olive oil for the bacon fat and vegetable broth for the chicken broth.

IN A LARGE saucepan, melt the butter over medium heat. Add the bacon and cook until crisp, about 4 minutes. Remove to a paper towel–lined plate and reserve.

Add the leeks to the fat in the pot and cook, stirring occasionally, until wilted, about 4 minutes. Add the squash and thyme and season with the nutmeg and some salt. Toss to coat the squash in the fat. Add the chicken broth and bring to a simmer. Add the apple chunks, cover, and simmer until the squash and apples are very tender when pierced with a fork, about 20 minutes.

In batches, puree the soup with ¼ cup of the sour cream in a blender (or with a handheld immersion blender right in the pot). Thin the remaining ¼ cup sour cream with 1 to 2 tablespoons milk, just enough to make it drizzle.

To serve, ladle the soup into warmed soup bowls. Drizzle each serving with some of the sour cream and top with the reserved bacon.

Kale and Kielbasa Soup

SERVES 6 WITH LEFTOVERS

3 tablespoons extra-virgin olive oil, plus more for drizzling

1 pound kielbasa, cut into ½-inch chunks

2 medium leeks, white and light green parts, halved and sliced

1 tablespoon chopped fresh thyme

2 cloves garlic, chopped

1½ teaspoons paprika

¼ teaspoon ground allspice

Big pinch crushed red pepper flakes

1 (14½-ounce) can diced tomatoes, with their juices

1½ quarts low-sodium chicken broth

2 bay leaves

Kosher salt

Freshly ground black pepper

2 medium russet potatoes, peeled and chopped

1 large bunch kale, tough stems trimmed and leaves chopped (about 8 ounces or 8 cups chopped leaves)

Grated Parmesan cheese, for serving

Kale is one of the most nutritious vegetables you can eat. And I love it. Every Wednesday is canasta card night in my house, and this is the perfect accompaniment! I serve the soup in deep bowls with chunks of warm crusty bread, pre-buttered and ready for dipping. It's a one-spoon meal.

HEAT A LARGE Dutch oven over medium heat and add the olive oil. When the oil is hot, add the kielbasa and cook and stir until browned all over, about 5 minutes. Add the leeks and thyme and cook until the leeks are wilted, about 6 minutes. Add the garlic, paprika, allspice, and red pepper flakes and cook until fragrant, about 1 minute. Add the tomatoes, chicken broth, and bay leaves and season with salt and pepper. Bring to a simmer, cover, and cook 30 minutes to develop the flavors.

Add the potatoes and kale. Simmer, uncovered, to reduce the soup and concentrate the flavors a bit, until the kale and potatoes are very tender, about 30 minutes. Remove the bay leaves and serve the soup with a final drizzle of olive oil and some grated Parmesan.

Roasted Brussels Sprouts
and Scallions

SERVES 6 OR MORE

2 pounds Brussels sprouts,
trimmed and halved

4 tablespoons extra-virgin olive oil

Kosher salt

Freshly ground black pepper

2 bunches scallions, trimmed
and cut into 1-inch lengths

Juice of ½ lemon

This is my husband David's favorite recipe. I bet he's sorry that he ever told me he loves Brussels sprouts. I prepare them so frequently that now, he gives me a look that says, "Again?" And I say yes! They are healthy! And they are the very best when roasted. But I have overroasted them more times than I care to count. Maybe that's why I get the look!

PREHEAT THE OVEN to 400°F. In a large bowl, toss the Brussels sprouts with 3 tablespoons of the olive oil and season with salt and pepper. Spread onto a rimmed baking sheet. Roast 20 minutes.

Add the scallions and drizzle with the remaining 1 table-spoon olive oil. Toss on the baking sheet to mix the scallions with the Brussels sprouts. Roast until the sprouts and scallions are browned and tender, about 20 minutes more, rotating and shaking the pan once or twice more to make sure all is browning evenly. Transfer to a platter, squeeze the lemon over the vegetables, and serve.

Corn off the Cob

SERVES 4 TO 6

1 tablespoon unsalted butter

4 slices bacon

1 medium red bell pepper, chopped

6 ears corn, kernels removed from the cob (about 3½ cups)

1 bunch scallions, trimmed and chopped (about 1 cup)

¼ teaspoon cayenne

¼ teaspoon granulated garlic

¼ teaspoon granulated onion

Kosher salt

Every year for the last 43 years, I've cut the corn off the cob in the summer and frozen enough for Thanksgiving and Christmas. That's a tradition! And it's an easy one for you to start in your family. It doesn't get any better, or healthier, than wonderfully fresh corn off the cob in the middle of winter. This is a recipe that I use at Christmas—the red bell pepper adds festive color.

IN A LARGE skillet over medium heat, melt the butter. Add the bacon and cook until crisp, about 5 minutes. Drain the bacon on paper towels, crumble, and set aside.

To the fat in the pan, add the bell pepper and cook until almost tender, about 5 minutes. Add the corn and scallions and season with the cayenne, granulated garlic, granulated onion, and some salt. Toss until the corn is cooked and the scallions are wilted, 3 to 4 minutes. Add back the bacon and toss for a minute or two to combine. Serve immediately.

"THE FIRST SUPERMARKET SUPPOSEDLY APPEARED ON THE AMERICAN LANDSCAPE IN 1946. THAT IS NOT VERY LONG AGO. UNTIL THEN, WHERE WAS ALL THE FOOD?"
—JOEL SALATIN

Holiday Stuffing

with Sausage, Pecans, and Apples

SERVES 8 OR MORE

9 tablespoons unsalted butter
(plus more for the baking dish)

8 ounces sage pork sausage, removed
from casings (a good-quality breakfast
sausage will work)

1 medium yellow onion, chopped

3 stalks celery, chopped

2 medium Golden Delicious apples,
peeled, cored, and cut into ½-inch chunks

1 cup coarsely chopped pecans

1 tablespoon chopped fresh thyme

1 tablespoon chopped fresh sage

3 cups low-sodium chicken broth,
plus more as needed

1 large egg

½ cup half-and-half

1 loaf day-old Pepperidge Farm sandwich
white bread with crust, cut into cubes
(about 14 cups)

Kosher salt

Freshly ground black pepper

You can use any kind of firm, good bread in this recipe. I like Pepperidge Farm's sandwich bread. You can even combine a few different kinds if you have some half loaves hanging around in the freezer. Leave the crusts on—it's less work and gives the stuffing some texture. A tip to prevent soggy stuffing: Let the bread dry out before you cook with it. Either remove the bread from the bag and leave it out all night, or put it in a 325°F oven for a half hour.

If you're cooking for a crowd, make extra stuffing. You'll be glad you did. This stuffing is versatile and can be used with the holiday recipes in this book or any season throughout the year—it's great under chicken or fish.

PREHEAT THE OVEN to 375°F. Generously butter a shallow 3-quart baking dish. In a large skillet, melt the butter over medium heat, pour off about 3 tablespoons into a small bowl, and set aside. Add the sausage to the skillet and cook, crumbling with a wooden spoon, until no longer pink, about 3 minutes. Add the onion and celery and cook, stirring occasionally, until the onion is slightly wilted, about 6 minutes. Add the apples, pecans, thyme, and sage and stir to coat everything with the butter. Add the chicken broth and bring to a simmer. Simmer until the apples are just tender, about 8 minutes. Scrape into a large bowl.

In a small bowl, beat the egg with the half-and-half. Add the bread to the bowl with the sausage mixture and pour the egg mixture over it. Season with salt and pepper and toss well to moisten all of the bread, adding a little more broth if necessary. Spread in the prepared baking dish, drizzle with the remaining melted butter, and tent with foil (don't let the foil touch the stuffing). Bake until heated through, about 20 minutes. Uncover and bake until the top is browned and crisp, about 30 minutes more.

Parker House Rolls

MAKES 32 SMALL ROLLS

1¼ cups whole milk

2 tablespoons unsalted butter, softened

2 tablespoons shortening

2 tablespoons sugar, plus a pinch

1 large egg

1½ teaspoons kosher salt

1 package active dry yeast, about 2¼ teaspoons

4 cups all-purpose flour, plus more as needed

Vegetable oil for greasing the bowl

4 tablespoons unsalted butter, melted and cooled, for brushing the rolls

Coarse flaky salt, for sprinkling

Grammy Carl made the best yeast rolls I've ever eaten, but unfortunately, I never paid attention to how she made them. But I think this recipe comes close. If not, go to the store, and in the freezer section you will find frozen dough—do not hesitate to use it!

IN A SMALL saucepan over low heat, combine 1 cup of the milk, the 2 tablespoons softened butter, and the shortening. Heat over medium heat just to melt the butter and shortening, then set it aside to cool completely. When cool, whisk in the 2 tablespoons sugar, the egg, and salt.

Meanwhile, add the remaining ¼ cup milk to a spouted measuring cup and gently heat in the microwave in short bursts until just warm to the touch (a little warmer than body temperature, about 100°F). Stir the yeast and the pinch of sugar into the warm milk. Let rest and rise about 5 minutes. Make sure it bubbles; that ensures the yeast is alive.

Combine the cooled milk mixture and the yeast mixture in a mixer fitted with the paddle attachment. Add

3½ cups of the flour and mix until a dough comes together. Switch to the dough hook, add the remaining ½ cup flour, and mix until a sticky dough forms, adding a little more flour or water, if necessary, so the dough forms a ball around the hook. Knead on medium-high speed until the dough is soft, springy, and smooth, 4 to 5 minutes. It should no longer stick to the sides of the bowl (add more flour, a tablespoon at a time, if it does). Oil a large bowl and transfer the dough to the bowl. Turn the dough in the bowl to coat in oil, cover with a dish towel, and let rise at room temperature until doubled, about 1 to 2 hours, depending on the temperature of the room.

Punch the dough down and divide into 4 equal pieces. Divide each of the 4 pieces into 8 small pieces, roll into balls, and put them in an 8- by 8-inch buttered pan. Cover the rolls loosely with a sheet of plastic wrap and let rise again until doubled, about 45 minutes.

Preheat the oven to 400°F. Lightly brush the rolls with the 4 tablespoons melted butter and sprinkle lightly with coarse salt. Bake until golden brown on the tops and bottoms, 22 to 25 minutes. Let the rolls cool on a rack for about 5 minutes, then transfer the pan to the table and let guests pull off the hot rolls.

Nita's Apple Pate

SERVES 8 OR MORE AS AN HORS D'OEUVRE

½ cup (1 stick) unsalted butter

½ small onion, finely chopped (about ½ cup)

2 small Golden Delicious apples: 1 peeled, cored, and chopped into ½-inch chunks and the other saved for garnish

1 pound chicken livers, trimmed of all fat and sinew, washed, and dried well

1 tablespoon chopped fresh thyme leaves

1 clove garlic, chopped

Kosher salt

Freshly ground black pepper

¼ cup Calvados, other apple brandy, or just regular brandy

1 tablespoon heavy cream, plus more as needed

2 tablespoons unsalted butter, melted

Juice of ½ lemon

This is a fabulous pate. I served it for many, many years at many, many cocktail parties and the serving dish was always empty at the end of the night. My daughter Nita, another apple of our eye, always wanted a taste when she was young. The melted butter on top at the end helps seal the pate and keep it from turning a darker color on top, but you can omit it if you want.

IN A LARGE skillet over medium heat, melt 4 tablespoons of the butter. Add the onion and the chopped apple and cook, stirring occasionally, until the onion and apple are soft and golden, 10 to 12 minutes.

Add the chicken livers, thyme, and garlic and season with salt and pepper. Cook and stir until the chicken livers are no longer pink on the outside, but not yet firm to the touch, about 3 minutes.

Add the Calvados and increase the heat to reduce the brandy to a glaze on the livers, about 3 minutes. The chicken livers should be cooked through, but still soft. Remove from the heat and let cool for 5 minutes.

Scrape the mixture into a food processor and add the remaining 4 tablespoons butter, cut into pieces, and 1 tablespoon cream. Process until very smooth, adding a little more cream if needed to get it nice and smooth. Pack into a large ramekin and pour the melted butter over the top to evenly cover the pate. Cover with plastic wrap and chill until firm, about 4 hours or overnight. When you are ready to serve, slice the remaining apple and squeeze fresh lemon juice on the slices to prevent discoloration. Serve the pate on a French baguette or crackers of your choice, garnished with the apple slices.

"NATURAL FORCES WITHIN US ARE THE
TRUE HEALERS OF DISEASE."

—HIPPOCRATES

Big Boy Bass

SERVES 4

1 teaspoon paprika

½ teaspoon granulated garlic

½ teaspoon granulated onion

4 skin-on bass fillets (about 2 pounds)

Kosher salt

Freshly ground black pepper

2 tablespoons extra-virgin olive oil

3 cloves garlic, thinly sliced

Juice of ½ lemon, plus a whole lemon, cut into wedges

½ cup dry white wine

4 tablespoons cold unsalted butter, cut into pieces

2 tablespoons chopped fresh Italian parsley

While my son was growing up, he always caught trout in the pond near our home. Then he moved away and came back several years later, like all good sons! When he returned, he went fishing in the pond and caught a bass. If you don't have a fisherman bringing you bass, go to the store and ask for the center-cut fillet from the bass—it will be thicker and cook more evenly.

IN A SMALL bowl, stir together the paprika, granulated garlic, and granulated onion. Sprinkle the spice mixture on the flesh side of the bass then season on both sides with salt and pepper.

Heat a large nonstick skillet over medium-high heat and add 1 tablespoon of the olive oil. When the oil is just beginning to smoke, add the bass, skin side down, and cook until the skin is very crisp, 3 to 4 minutes. Carefully flip the fillets and cook on the other side until the fish is just cooked through, 3 to 4 minutes more. Put the fillets on serving plates, skin side up. The skin makes a beautiful crust that you'll want to see.

Carefully pour the oil out of the skillet and wipe it clean with a paper towel. Return the skillet to medium-high heat and add the remaining 1 tablespoon olive oil. Add the sliced garlic and cook, stirring, until just golden, about 1 minute (don't let it burn!). Add the lemon juice and white wine and boil to reduce by about half. Drop in the butter pieces, a few at a time, whisking to incorporate and make a creamy sauce. Stir in the parsley, pour over the fish, and serve with lemon wedges.

Cast-Iron
Filet Mignon Sandwiches

MAKES 2 SANDWICHES

2 (6-ounce) filet mignons
(about 2 inches thick), tied by your butcher

Kosher salt

Freshly ground black pepper

4 tablespoons plus 2 teaspoons
unsalted butter

2 tablespoons extra-virgin olive oil

1 clove garlic, smashed and peeled

2 leeks, white and light green parts,
halved and thinly sliced

2 teaspoons chopped fresh tarragon

½ cup dry red wine

1 teaspoon truffle oil

2 brioche buns, halved

This recipe is decadent. It can make for a won-derful dinner for two or a very fancy picnic lunch. David and I indulged in these sandwiches on an episode of *Farmhouse Rules* and I've yearned for them ever since. This is my friend Kitty's recipe. Thank you, Kitty!

SEASON THE FILETS generously with salt and pepper. In a medium cast-iron skillet over medium-high heat, melt 2 tablespoons of the butter with the olive oil and garlic. When the butter begins to bubble, add the filet mignon pieces. Tip the skillet slightly and baste the tops with the butter and olive oil. Cook until deeply browned on the bottom, about 3 minutes. Flip and continue cooking and basting on the other side until brown, about 3 minutes. Turn the pieces on their sides and sear the edges until brown. Remove from the skillet and let the steak rest while you prepare the leeks and sauce.

Add the leeks and 2 tablespoons of the butter to the skillet and sauté until the leeks are soft, about 4 minutes. Add the tarragon. Turn the heat to high and add the red wine. Let the sauce reduce by half, 2 to 3 minutes. Lower the heat to simmer and stir in the truffle oil.

Heat a large skillet over medium-high heat. Spread the remaining 2 teaspoons butter onto the brioche buns and place in the pan until slightly browned, about 2 minutes.

To serve, slice the filet mignon against the grain and place on one half of each brioche bun. Top with some leeks and their sauce and the other half of each bun and serve immediately.

Venison Chili
from the Land

SERVES 6

2 tablespoons extra-virgin olive oil

4 slices bacon, chopped

2 pounds venison stew meat, cut into
1- or 2-inch chunks

Kosher salt

Freshly ground black pepper

1 medium onion, chopped

1 red bell pepper, chopped

1 (4-ounce) can chopped green
chilies, drained

3 cloves garlic, chopped

1 tablespoon chili powder

2 teaspoons cumin

1 teaspoon paprika (preferably smoked)

¼ teaspoon chipotle chili powder

1 cup dark beer (such as Dos Equis)

1 (28-ounce) can fire-roasted whole
tomatoes, crushed by hand

1 (14½-ounce) can low-sodium beef broth

1 chipotle chili in adobo, chopped,
plus 2 tablespoons sauce from the can

2 tablespoons light brown sugar

2 tablespoons unsweetened cocoa powder

Our local Hudson Valley Bounty organization sponsors a chili contest every year on the Hudson riverfront and my son won two years in a row with his venison chili. But this is not his exact recipe—he thinks he's special now and doesn't want anyone else to win, so he won't share it! Instead, this recipe is *my* take on venison chili, and it's really a cross between a chili and a stew. It would be great served with rice, corn or flour tortillas, or just a big chunk of corn bread. I think my son and I should compete against each other next year!

HEAT A LARGE Dutch oven over medium heat. Add the olive oil and bacon and cook until the bacon renders its fat, about 4 minutes. Remove the bacon to a paper towel–lined plate to drain.

Pat the venison dry with paper towels and season with salt and pepper. In batches, cook the meat in the Dutch oven until browned all over, about 6 minutes per batch. Remove the meat to a plate as it browns.

Once all of the meat is out of the pot, add the onion, bell pepper, green chilies, and garlic and cook until the onion and pepper begin to soften, about 5 minutes. Add the chili powder, cumin, paprika, and chipotle powder and cook until the vegetables are coated with the spices, about 1 minute. Pour in the beer, bring to a boil, and boil until reduced by half, about 2 minutes. Add the tomatoes, beef broth, chopped chipotle and chipotle sauce, brown sugar, and cocoa powder. Bring to a simmer and add the bacon and venison back. Simmer the stew, partially covered, until the meat is tender and the sauce is thick and flavorful, about 1½ hours. If the meat is tender but the sauce is too thin, simmer rapidly over high heat for a minute or two to reduce, stirring to keep the bottom from burning.

Heavenly Hash

SERVES 4

3 tablespoons unsalted butter

2 slices bacon, chopped

1 small onion, chopped

1 small carrot, chopped

2 medium russet potatoes (about 1¼ pounds), cut into small chunks

1 tablespoon chopped fresh thyme

1 teaspoon paprika

Pinch freshly grated nutmeg

Kosher salt

Freshly ground black pepper

2 cups diced leftover meat

1 cup frozen peas

½ cup low-sodium beef broth

1 to 2 tablespoons Worcestershire sauce

¼ cup chopped fresh Italian parsley

This is another farmer-friendly recipe that is easy and tasty. It's great for leftover meat—chicken, beef, venison, lamb, or whatever you have around. Add mashed potatoes and call it dinner. If you're making it for breakfast or brunch, add poached or fried eggs on top.

MELT THE BUTTER in a large cast-iron skillet over medium-low heat. Add the bacon, onion, and carrot and cook until the fat is rendered and the onion is softened, about 8 minutes. Add the potatoes, increase the heat to medium, and cook until the potatoes begin to soften and the vegetables are well browned, about 10 minutes.

Add the thyme, paprika, and nutmeg and season with salt and pepper. Add the diced meat, peas, beef broth, and Worcestershire to taste and simmer until the vegetables are very tender, about 3 minutes.

Increase the heat to high to boil away any excess liquid and glaze the hash with the meat juices, about 5 minutes, flipping and pressing parts of the hash every so often to brown and crisp it all. Stir in the parsley and serve.

Turkey Carcass Creations

SERVES 6

1 leftover Thanksgiving turkey carcass, with a little meat still clinging to it

2 large carrots, 1 coarsely chopped, 1 diced

4 stalks celery, 2 coarsely chopped, 2 diced

1 large onion, coarsely chopped

5 sprigs fresh sage

5 sprigs fresh thyme

5 sprigs fresh parsley, plus ¼ cup chopped

2 bay leaves

1 quart low-sodium chicken broth

2 medium leeks, white and light green parts, halved and sliced

Grated zest of 1 lemon, removed with a vegetable peeler

1½ cups (8 ounces) wide egg noodles

Kosher salt

Freshly ground black pepper

I always make this soup after Thanksgiving since it's a great use of the turkey carcass. Sometimes I also throw in a little leftover gravy, stuffing, and maybe some leftover vegetables. They dissolve into the soup and add tons of flavor. You can make the soup at other times of the year with the carcass from a roasted chicken.

PICK OFF ANY meat from the turkey carcass and chop. Refrigerate it while you make the soup. Hack the carcass into 3 or 4 pieces, using a large chef's knife and kitchen shears when the going gets tough on your hands! Put the carcass in a large pot and add the coarsely chopped carrot, celery, and onion, the sprigs of sage, thyme, and parsley, and the bay leaves. Add the broth and pour in enough water to cover the carcass, about 6 cups. Bring to a simmer, cover, and cook until the stock has reduced a bit and is very flavorful, about 1½ hours. Strain and discard the solids. You should have about 8 cups stock.

Wipe out the soup pot and pour the stock back in. Add the diced carrot and celery, the sliced leeks, and the lemon zest strips. Simmer until the vegetables are tender, about 20 minutes. Add the reserved turkey meat and the egg noodles and simmer until the noodles are tender, about 8 to 10 minutes. Stir in the chopped parsley, remove the lemon zest, and serve. Be sure to taste for salt and pepper.

"I Love Leftover Turkey Time"
Sandwiches

MAKES 2 SANDWICHES

2 tablespoons mayonnaise

2 tablespoons leftover cranberry sauce

1 tablespoon grainy Dijon mustard

2 tablespoons unsalted butter, softened

4 slices sturdy country white
bread or rye

4 slices leftover Thanksgiving turkey (page 187)

½ cup leftover stuffing (page 163)

4 slices avocado

4 thin slices sharp Cheddar or Brie cheese
(or use whatever is in the refrigerator!)

My daughter Kimberlee and her family refer to my sandwiches as Gigi sandwiches. I make them whenever they come for lunch. I usually grill them and add sliced avocado to make them even moister. If you have leftover gravy, warm some up and use it as a dip along with the cranberry mayo!

When I don't have turkey on hand, I use whatever is in the fridge—leftover pork roast (page 181), prime rib (page 42), roast chicken (page 34), or even canned tuna.

IN A SMALL bowl, stir together the mayonnaise, cranberry sauce, and mustard. Spread the butter on one side of all of the bread slices. Flip 2 slices of bread, buttered sides down, in a skillet. Spread each with a little of the cranberry mayo. Layer the turkey on top, then the stuffing, avocado, and cheese. Spread a little more of the cranberry spread on top of the cheese. Add the second slices of bread, turn the heat to medium, and place the skillet on the burner. Grill until the sandwiches are golden on both sides, 4 minutes. Cut the sandwiches in half and serve with the remaining cranberry mayo sauce.

"NO ONE WHO COOKS, COOKS ALONE. EVEN AT HER
MOST SOLITARY, A COOK IN THE KITCHEN IS
SURROUNDED BY GENERATIONS OF COOKS PAST,
THE ADVICE AND MENUS OF COOKS PRESENT, THE WISDOM
OF COOKBOOK WRITERS."
—LAURIE COLWIN

Basic Bone-In Pork Roast

SERVES 4 TO 6

1 (4½-pound) bone-in center-cut
pork loin roast, tied by your butcher

2 teaspoons paprika (preferably smoked)

1 teaspoon granulated garlic

1 teaspoon granulated onion

Kosher salt

Freshly ground black pepper

3 tablespoons extra-virgin olive oil

1 large onion, sliced

2 Golden Delicious apples, peeled,
cored, and cut into big chunks

1½ pounds sauerkraut, rinsed and drained well

1 tablespoon chopped fresh thyme

4 cloves garlic, smashed and peeled

2 bay leaves

1 cup hard cider

3 tablespoons light brown sugar

1 cup low-sodium chicken broth

2 tablespoons unsalted butter

Another farmhouse favorite. My kids always loved it. The guests love it. And there are never any leftovers when I serve it.

PREHEAT THE OVEN to 400°F. Pat the roast dry and sprinkle all over with 1 teaspoon of the paprika, ½ teaspoon of the granulated garlic, ½ teaspoon of the granulated onion, and some salt and pepper. Heat half of the olive oil in a large Dutch oven over medium-high heat. Add the pork and brown on all sides, about 6 minutes. Transfer to a plate.

Add the remaining olive oil to the pot. Add the sliced onion and cook, stirring, until wilted and light golden, about 5 minutes. Add the apples and sauerkraut and cook until the sauerkraut begins to brown on the edges, about 4 minutes. Season with the remaining 1 teaspoon

paprika, ½ teaspoon granulated garlic, and ½ teaspoon granulated onion and some salt and pepper (easy on the salt, sauerkraut is salty on its own). Add the thyme, garlic, and bay leaves. Increase the heat to high and add the hard cider. Bring to a boil and cook until reduced by half, about 2 minutes. Add the brown sugar and chicken broth and return to a simmer. Put the pork, bone side down, on top of the sauerkraut and cover the pot. Transfer to the oven and bake until the pork reaches 145°F on an instant-read thermometer, about 45 minutes. Remove the pork to a cutting board and let rest for 10 minutes.

Meanwhile, bring the sauerkraut and cooking juices to a boil over medium-high heat. Whisk in the butter and boil until the juices thicken slightly, about 2 minutes. Discard the bay leaves. Carve the pork roast and serve on a bed of the sauerkraut and apples.

Fruited Pork Medley

SERVES 6

2½ pounds boneless pork shoulder, cut into 1½-inch chunks

Kosher salt

Freshly ground black pepper

¾ cup all-purpose flour

4 tablespoons extra-virgin olive oil

2 medium onions, cut into 1-inch chunks

2 large carrots, cut into 1-inch chunks

2 teaspoons chopped fresh thyme

2 teaspoons paprika

2 teaspoons ground cumin

1 teaspoon ground coriander

½ teaspoon ground ginger

¼ teaspoon ground cinnamon

3 cloves garlic, finely chopped

1 cup amber beer

½ cup apple cider

3½ cups low-sodium chicken broth

2 bay leaves

½ cup halved dried apricots

½ cup halved pitted prunes

¼ cup golden raisins

¼ cup chopped fresh Italian parsley

2 tablespoons grainy mustard

This is a wonderfully fragrant fall dish. The flavors are complex, so it's best to keep the side dishes simple. It would be excellent served with basmati rice and a simple green salad.

If you have leftovers, it's even better the next day!

SEASON THE PORK with salt and pepper. In a large bowl, toss the pork in the flour to lightly coat, tapping off any excess. Heat a large Dutch oven over medium-high heat and add 2 tablespoons of the olive oil. When the oil is hot, add half of the pork and brown on all sides, about 4 minutes. Transfer the pork to a plate. Use the remaining 2 tablespoons of olive oil to brown the second batch and transfer to the plate. Reserve 2 tablespoons of the flour.

When all of the pork is out of the pot, reduce the heat to medium, add the onions and carrots, and season with salt and pepper. Cook, stirring occasionally, until the onions begin to caramelize on the edges, about 5 minutes. Add the thyme, paprika, cumin, coriander, ginger, and cinnamon and sprinkle with the 2 tablespoons reserved flour. Toss to coat the vegetables in the flour and cook, stirring occasionally, until the flour is browned on the surface of the vegetables, about 1 minute. Add the garlic and cook until fragrant, about 1 minute. Increase the heat to medium high and pour in the beer and apple cider. Boil until reduced by half, about 2 minutes. Add the chicken broth and bay leaves and adjust the heat to a simmer. Add the pork, cover, and simmer until the pork is tender, about 1 hour.

Add the apricots, prunes, and raisins. Simmer rapidly, uncovered, until the fruit is plump and tender and the stew is thickened to your liking, about 10 minutes. Discard the bay leaves. Stir in the parsley, whisk in the mustard, and serve.

Stuffed Cabbage
Without the Roll

SERVES 6

3 tablespoons extra-virgin olive oil

1½ pounds ground pork (or beef)

1 medium onion, chopped

1 medium carrot, chopped

½ medium head savoy cabbage, shredded (about 8 cups)

2 teaspoons paprika

¼ teaspoon allspice

Pinch cayenne pepper

3 cups low-sodium chicken broth

1 (28-ounce) can whole tomatoes in juice, crushed by hand

3 tablespoons cider vinegar

3 tablespoons light brown sugar

2 teaspoons Worcestershire sauce

½ cup long grain rice

Kosher salt

3 tablespoons chopped fresh dill

Sour cream, for serving

I love all the ingredients in cabbage rolls, but I've never really enjoyed the roll aspect. So instead, I take all the ingredients and chop-chop-them-in-the-pot to make a wonderful cabbage stew. Adding the rice at the end ensures that all the great spices are absorbed and come through in every bite. Plus, cabbage is an excellent source of fiber and nutrients. This is a great recipe to warm you up on one of those chilly autumn days.

HEAT THE OLIVE oil in a large Dutch oven over medium-high heat. Add the pork and cook until no longer pink, about 5 minutes. Add the onion, carrot, and cabbage. Sprinkle with the paprika, allspice, and cayenne. Cook until the cabbage is wilted, about 5 minutes.

Add the broth, tomatoes, vinegar, brown sugar, and Worcestershire. Bring to a simmer and cook until the cabbage is tender, about 40 minutes.

Add the rice and season with salt. Cook until the rice is just tender (it will cook more off the heat), about 15 minutes. Stir in the chopped dill. Serve in soup bowls, with dollops of sour cream.

Pot Roast Done Easy

SERVES 6 PLUS LEFTOVERS

1 (3-pound) boneless beef chuck roast, tied by your butcher

½ teaspoon granulated garlic

½ teaspoon granulated onion

Kosher salt

Freshly ground black pepper

All-purpose flour, for dredging

3 tablespoons extra-virgin olive oil

2 medium onions, sliced

2 tablespoons tomato paste

1½ cups dry red wine

1 quart low-sodium beef broth

2 sprigs fresh thyme

2 sprigs fresh rosemary

2 bay leaves

3 large carrots, cut into big chunks

3 stalks celery, cut into big chunks

1½ pounds red potatoes, cut into big chunks

¼ cup chopped fresh Italian parsley

This pot roast was a very popular dish in my home, my restaurant, and with all my catering clients.

After the meat has cooked through, I will sometimes put the vegetables and broth in a food processor and pulse until a gravy texture is achieved. Then I slice the meat, pour the gravy over it, and serve with mashed potatoes.

PREHEAT THE OVEN to 350°F. Season the roast all over with the granulated garlic, granulated onion, salt, and pepper. Dredge the roast on all sides in flour. Reserve 3 tablespoons of the flour. Heat a large Dutch oven over medium heat and add the olive oil. When the oil is hot, brown the roast on all sides, about 10 minutes in all. Transfer the roast to a plate.

Add the onions to the pot and cook, stirring occasionally, until light golden and wilted, about 8 minutes. Add the tomato paste and stir until it melts into the onions, about 2 minutes. Sprinkle the onion mixture with the 3 tablespoons reserved flour and cook until it coats the onion. Add the wine and simmer until reduced by half, about 3 minutes. Add the beef broth, thyme, rosemary, and bay leaves. Bring to a simmer and return the roast to the pot. (The liquid should come about halfway up the sides of the meat.) Cover and bake in the oven, turning the roast once, for 1½ hours.

Add the carrots, celery, and potatoes, cover, and bake until the roast is very tender all the way through and the vegetables are soft, 45 minutes to 1 hour more.

Remove the roast to a cutting board and let rest for 10 minutes. Meanwhile, stir the parsley into the sauce and simmer rapidly over medium-high heat to reduce to your liking. Discard the bay leaves and herb sprigs. Put all of the liquid in a food processor and pulse until a gravy texture is achieved. Remove the strings, thinly slice the meat, and pour gravy over.

Thanks for Giving
Turkey with Gravy

SERVES 8, WITH LEFTOVERS

TURKEY

½ cup (1 stick) unsalted butter, softened

1 (15- to 16-pound) turkey,
at room temperature

1 tablespoon granulated garlic

1 tablespoon granulated onion

Kosher salt

Freshly ground black pepper

1 bunch fresh sage

1 medium onion, quartered

2 cups low-sodium chicken broth,
plus more, as needed, for the gravy

GRAVY

½ cup all-purpose flour

1 teaspoon dried poultry seasoning

Better than Bouillon (brand) chicken-
flavored gravy base

There is a multitude of ways to make a turkey, and I have tried them all. This is just one way, and it's one of my favorites. I've been cooking Thanksgiving dinner for as long as I can remember and have probably never had less than 22 people at the table. But this recipe calls for a smaller bird than I normally use. Take the turkey out of the refrigerator 3 hours before you want to put it in the oven to allow it to come to room temperature, especially since it could be slightly frozen inside but you won't know it. After you've enjoyed this wonderful turkey, you can make Turkey Carcass Creations (page 177), "I Love Leftover Turkey Time" Sandwiches (page 178), or just put a piece of turkey on a Parker House roll.

PREHEAT THE OVEN to 400°F with a rack in the lower third. Rub the softened butter all over the turkey. Sprinkle granulated garlic, granulated onion, salt, and pepper all over the outside of the bird. Season the inside with salt and pepper. Add sage and the quartered onion to the cavity. Place the turkey on a rack in a roasting pan. Pour 1 cup of broth in the bottom of the pan. Roast the turkey uncovered for 30 minutes.

Reduce the oven temperature to 325°F and pour in 1 cup broth. Continue to roast 4 hours and check the temperature in the thickest part of the leg and thigh (it must read 165°F).

Remove the turkey to a cutting board and let rest for 20 minutes before carving. Using the liquid from the roasting pan, put ½ cup of liquid and ½ cup of flour in a bowl and whisk until smooth. Set aside. Place the roasting pan on the stove over medium heat. Add the flour mixture to the liquid in the pan, whisking constantly, and bring to a boil. Cook 3 minutes. Season with poultry seasoning and Better than Bouillon to taste. Add water or more broth if the gravy is too thick or you need more liquid.

Carve the turkey and serve with the gravy.

One-Dish
Chicken Macaroni Casserole

SERVES 6 TO 8

....

8 ounces elbow macaroni

6 tablespoons unsalted butter
(plus more for the baking dish)

8 ounces cremini mushrooms, thickly sliced

Kosher salt

Freshly ground black pepper

1 bunch scallions, white and light
green parts, chopped (about 1 cup)

2 teaspoons chopped fresh thyme

1 clove garlic, finely chopped

5 tablespoons all-purpose flour

2 tablespoons dry white wine

3 cups low-sodium chicken broth

1 cup half-and-half

Generous pinch freshly grated nutmeg

3 cups chopped boneless, skinless
rotisserie chicken meat (or other leftover
cooked chicken or turkey)

1½ cups (8 ounces) frozen peas and
carrots, thawed

¼ cup chopped fresh Italian parsley

4 ounces cream cheese, cut into
chunks and softened

¼ cup fine dry breadcrumbs

¼ cup grated Parmesan cheese

....

I love finding ways to use leftovers and this recipe is one of my favorites. Be sure to use freshly grated nutmeg—combined with the fresh thyme and mushrooms, it creates such an amazing aroma that your guests will be drooling before you pull the casserole out of the oven.

BRING A LARGE pot of salted water to a boil for the pasta. Preheat the oven to 400°F. Butter a 9- by 13-inch baking dish. When the water is boiling, add the elbow macaroni and cook until very al dente, several minutes shy of the package cooking time. Drain, rinse, and pat dry and put in a large bowl.

In a large saucepan over medium heat, melt 4 tablespoons of the butter. Add the mushrooms and season with salt and pepper. Cook until the mushrooms have given up their liquid. Increase the heat to boil away any excess liquid, about 5 minutes. Add the scallions,

thyme, and garlic and cook until the scallions are wilted, about 3 minutes.

Sprinkle the vegetables with the flour and cook, stirring, until lightly browned, about 1 minute. Add the wine and cook until just absorbed. Pour in the chicken broth and half-and-half. Bring to a simmer and season with salt, pepper, and the nutmeg. Simmer until the sauce is thickened and has lost the raw flour taste, about 7 minutes. Stir in the chicken, peas and carrots, and parsley and simmer just to heat the chicken through. Off the heat, whisk in the cream cheese until smooth.

Pour the chicken and sauce into the bowl with the macaroni and toss well. Spread into the prepared baking dish. In a small bowl, toss together the breadcrumbs and Parmesan. Sprinkle the breadcrumbs over the top of the baking dish. Dot the top with the remaining 2 tablespoons butter, cut into small pieces. Bake until the casserole is very bubbly and the top is crispy and golden brown, about 25 minutes.

Sausage Pasta Casserole

SERVES 6

1 pound rigatoni

2 tablespoons extra-virgin olive oil (plus more for the baking dish)

1 pound sweet Italian sausage, removed from the casings

1 medium onion, sliced

1 medium bulb fennel, trimmed, cored, and sliced

3 cloves garlic, chopped

¼ teaspoon crushed red pepper flakes

1 (28-ounce) can whole tomatoes, crushed by hand

Kosher salt

½ cup heavy cream

½ cup fresh basil leaves, coarsely chopped

2 cups (8 ounces) shredded mozzarella cheese

½ cup grated Parmesan cheese

Fennel is a great aromatic ingredient that I love to use with sausage. There's something about the spices in a sweet Italian sausage that pair so nicely with the fennel. Make sure to keep the casserole in the oven until the cheese is nice and toasted on top—delicious!

PREHEAT THE OVEN to 425°F. Brush a shallow 3-quart baking dish with olive oil. Bring a large pot of salted water to a boil. Cook the pasta until very al dente; you still want it to retain a little bite. Drain well.

Meanwhile, in a large Dutch oven over medium-high heat, add the olive oil. When the oil is hot, add the sausage and cook and crumble with a wooden spoon until no longer pink, about 4 minutes. Add the onion and fennel and cook until softened, about 10 minutes. Add the garlic and red pepper flakes and cook until the garlic is fragrant, about 1 minute. Add the tomatoes and season with salt. Bring to a simmer and add the cream; if the sauce is too thick, add a little water from the pasta. Turn up the heat to medium high and simmer rapidly to thicken the sauce and blend the flavors, about 10 minutes.

Add the rigatoni and basil and toss to coat the pasta with the sauce. Remove from the heat and stir in half of the mozzarella and Parmesan. Transfer the mixture to the prepared baking dish and sprinkle with the remaining mozzarella and Parmesan. Bake until browned and bubbly, 15 to 20 minutes.

Farmer's Favorite
Molasses Ginger Cookies

MAKES ABOUT 2½ DOZEN COOKIES

2 cups all-purpose flour

2 teaspoons baking soda

2 teaspoons ground ginger

1 teaspoon ground cinnamon

¼ teaspoon ground cloves

¼ teaspoon ground nutmeg

½ teaspoon fine salt

6 tablespoons vegetable shortening, softened

6 tablespoons unsalted butter, softened

1 cup packed light brown sugar

¼ cup molasses

1 large egg

½ cup finely chopped crystallized ginger (optional)

Granulated sugar, for rolling the cookies

I add crystallized ginger to these molasses cookies because I love the surprising burst of flavor and the two different textures. I love a good chewy bit, but if you don't, just leave the crystallized ginger out! Don't overbake the cookies, they aren't very forgiving. But, if you *do*, make a cup of tea or warm a mug of cider and dunk, dunk, dunk!

SIFT THE FLOUR, baking soda, ground ginger, cinnamon, cloves, nutmeg, and salt onto a piece of parchment paper or waxed paper.

In a mixer fitted with the paddle attachment, cream the shortening, butter, and brown sugar on high speed until light and fluffy, about 2 minutes. Add the molasses and egg and beat until smooth. Pour in the flour mixture and beat on low, just to combine. Add the crystallized ginger, if using, and mix just to combine. Cover the dough and chill in the refrigerator until firm, about 2 hours.

Preheat the oven to 350°F and line two baking sheets with parchment.

Spread about a cup of granulated sugar on a large plate. Form the chilled dough into walnut-size balls and roll in the sugar. Space the cookies an inch or so apart on the lined baking sheets, leaving room for them to spread. Bake, rotating the pans from top to bottom halfway through, until the cookies are puffed and the edges are set but the centers are still soft, 10 to 12 minutes. Let cool on the baking sheets a few minutes, then remove to a rack to cool completely. Proceed with the remaining dough until all of the cookies are baked. Pay attention to the first batch of cookies and make sure they are baked to your satisfaction. If not, adjust the oven temperature or the time.

Chocolate Every Single Day Cake

SERVES 8

CAKE

Unsalted butter, softened, for the baking pan

2 cups all-purpose flour (plus more for the baking pan)

½ cup natural cocoa

2 teaspoons baking soda

1 teaspoon baking powder

¼ teaspoon fine salt

1 cup sugar

1 cup sour cream

¾ cup vegetable oil

2 large eggs

1 teaspoon vanilla extract

1 cup boiling water

FROSTING

1 (12-ounce) bag chocolate chips

1 cup sour cream

1 teaspoon vanilla extract

½ cup confectioners' sugar

Pinch kosher salt

4 tablespoons unsalted butter, softened and cut into chunks

My carrot that I dangled in front of my kids every night: If you don't eat your dinner, you don't eat dessert. Simple rule. It worked. We always kept a slice of this chocolate cake for Kim in hopes that eventually she would eat her dinner. Thank goodness for our dog Toast, who would spend lots of time next to Kim under the table!

This cake mixes up in one bowl in just a few minutes, so you can make it at the spur of the moment. The frosting is optional, but a great addition if you have a couple of extra minutes to spare.

FOR THE CAKE, preheat the oven to 350°F. Butter and flour a 9- by 13-inch baking pan. Sift the flour, cocoa, baking soda, baking powder, and salt onto a piece of parchment paper.

In a large mixing bowl, whisk together the sugar, sour cream, vegetable oil, eggs, and vanilla until light and smooth. Whisk in the flour mixture just to combine. Whisk the boiling water into the batter just until smooth (don't overmix). Pour the batter into the prepared pan. Bake until a tester comes out clean, 35 to 40 minutes. Cool on a rack completely before frosting.

For the frosting, melt the chocolate chips in a bowl over a pan of simmering water. Transfer the melted chocolate to the bowl of a mixer and add the sour cream and vanilla. Beat on medium until smooth. Reduce the speed to low and add the confectioners' sugar and salt. Once it's combined, increase the speed to medium and beat in the butter, a chunk at a time, until smooth. Increase the speed to high and beat until fluffy and light.

Spread the frosting over the cooled cake.

Just the BEST Apple Pie

SERVES 8

....

PIE DOUGH

2¼ cups all-purpose flour (plus more for rolling)

1 cup (2 sticks) cold unsalted butter,
cut into ½-inch pieces

1 teaspoon sugar

¼ teaspoon kosher salt

1 cup (4 ounces) shredded
extra-sharp white Cheddar cheese

FILLING

2 pounds, or 8 large, Granny Smith apples,
peeled and sliced into ¼-inch wedges

½ cup granulated sugar

¼ cup packed light brown sugar

¼ cup all-purpose flour

1 teaspoon ground cinnamon

½ teaspoon grated nutmeg

3 tablespoons unsalted butter,
sliced into pats

3 tablespoons cream

1 tablespoon granulated sugar,
for sprinkling

....

My dad always said that apple pie without cheese is like a kiss without a squeeze. And boy, did that cheese vary over the years! The first time my mother made this, she used Velveeta cheese (that was in the '50s). Over the years, the cheese got progressively more sophisticated and now, a local Cheddar is my cheese of choice.

Remember to bake the apple pie long enough—you don't want the apples to be crunchy. Otherwise, why bother to make a pie? I've used a Pillsbury crust before, but the fresh, home-made cheese crust recipe here is best, unless you're stressed!

FOR THE PIE dough, combine the flour, butter, sugar, and salt in the bowl of a food processor and give it quick pulses to blend the ingredients, until the mixture looks crumbly (crumbles should be the size of peas). Add the cheese and pulse again until combined and the cheese is worked into the mixture and cut into small chunks. Dump the mixture out into a bowl, drizzle in 6 tablespoons of ice cold water, and mix it in with a

fork until the flour is moistened and comes together as a dough. Add another tablespoon of water, if needed, to bring the dough together. Divide the dough in half, shape each half into a ball, and flatten to a disk. Wrap in plastic and refrigerate for 30 minutes.

For the filling, combine the Granny Smith apples, granulated sugar, brown sugar, flour, cinnamon, and nutmeg in a large bowl and toss to combine.

Preheat the oven to 425°F. Adjust the rack to the center of the oven. Roll out 1 disk of the dough on a *lightly* floured surface to a 12-inch round. Fit into a 9-inch pie plate. Add the apples and dot with the butter. Roll out the second dough round. Cover the top of the apples with the second pie round, pressing the edges of the two crust layers to seal. Trim the crust so you are left with a 1-inch overhang. Tuck the crust underneath itself so it's flush with the edge of the pie plate. Crimp the edges decoratively. Pat the pie with the cream and sprinkle with the granulated sugar. Make 5 air slits in the center of the pie. Bake until the crust is set, about 25 minutes.

Lower the oven temperature to 350°F and bake 50 minutes more, until the crust is golden brown. Cool on a rack before slicing.

Apple Cake

SERVES 8 OR MORE

....

1 tablespoon very soft unsalted butter

3 small Golden Delicious apples, peeled, cored, and cut into small chunks

¼ cup lightly packed light brown sugar

½ cup chopped toasted pecans

2 teaspoons ground cinnamon

Grated zest and juice of 1 medium orange (about 1 tablespoon zest and ½ cup juice)

3 cups all-purpose flour (plus more for the pan)

1 tablespoon baking powder

½ teaspoon ground allspice

½ teaspoon ground ginger

¼ teaspoon freshly grated nutmeg

¼ teaspoon fine salt

4 large eggs

1 cup vegetable oil

1¾ cups granulated sugar

1 teaspoon vanilla extract

....

This cake is easy to stir together and *always appropriate*—it's a great dessert but it's also not too sweet for breakfast or to enjoy with coffee or tea as an afternoon snack.

Wrapped in plastic, it keeps well for 2 or 3 days after baking. Of course, when my kids were growing up on the farm, or today when all my kids and grandkids are home, I'm lucky if two cakes last all day long! I have to watch them all like a hawk to make sure they don't eat it on the couch and get apple cake crumbs in the cushions. Now I remember why I had slipcovers made!

THE GROWTH OF AN APPLE.

THE FABRIC OF A FARMER.

PREHEAT THE OVEN to 350°F. Use the softened butter to thoroughly coat a 12-cup Bundt pan and then coat with flour, tapping out the excess.

In a large bowl, toss the apples with the brown sugar, pecans, 1 teaspoon of the cinnamon, and half of the orange juice. Let it sit while you mix the batter.

Sift the remaining 1 teaspoon cinnamon, the flour, baking powder, allspice, ginger, nutmeg, and salt onto a piece of parchment paper.

In a mixer fitted with the paddle attachment, combine the eggs, vegetable oil, granulated sugar, vanilla, and orange zest and remaining juice. Beat on medium speed until smooth. Pour in the sifted dry ingredients and mix on low just to blend.

Spread enough batter (about 1½ cups) to coat the bottom of the Bundt pan. Spread a little less than half of the apples over the batter. Top with half of the remaining batter. Top with the remaining apples, then finally spread over the remaining batter. Bake until a tester comes out almost clean, with just a crumb or two attached, 55 minutes to 1 hour. Cool on a rack for 10 minutes before inverting and unmolding the cake onto the rack to cool.

Peter Peter Pumpkin Pie

SERVES 8

PUMPKIN

1 medium sugar pumpkin (3 to 4 pounds
or 2 cups of puree)

Canola oil (or whatever oil you've got,
any will do), for oiling pumpkin

EASY PIE DOUGH

2 cups all-purpose flour (plus more for rolling)

¼ teaspoon kosher salt

⅔ cup (11 tablespoons) cold unsalted butter,
cut into ½-inch pieces

EASIER PIE DOUGH

Pillsbury. Red Package. Refrigeration section of the
supermarket. Fresh is best unless you're stressed.

FILLING

1 (14-ounce) can sweetened
condensed milk

½ cup heavy cream

3 large eggs

2 tablespoons cornstarch

2 tablespoons molasses

2 tablespoons canola oil
(or whatever oil you've got)

1 tablespoon ground cinnamon

1 teaspoon ground ginger

¼ teaspoon kosher salt

When you go to the pumpkin patch, make sure to pick a sugar pumpkin for this pie, as it has the best flavor and texture for baking.

Please remember to always taste the filling before you bake it: You may find that your cinnamon has lost its zip since the last time you used it and you need to add more. Or you might need to add a pinch more salt. If something tastes good in its uncooked state, it will taste phenomenal when it's cooked! Grammy Carl always had extra dough and made these little cinnamon tidbits with it: Whether you're using the easy or the easier pie dough, you can roll out the extra dough, dot with butter, and sprinkle with sugar and cinnamon. Roll the dough up, slice into rolls, and bake in the oven at 400°F for 10 minutes. Some like these better than the pie!

TO ROAST THE pumpkin, preheat the oven to 375°F. Line a baking sheet with foil. Remove the stem from the pumpkin and scrape out the insides, discarding the seeds. Cut the pumpkin in half and lay the pieces cut side down on the prepared baking sheet. Rub canola oil all over the skin. Roast until fork-tender, about 1 hour. Let cool.

For the pie dough, combine the flour and salt in a large bowl. Add the butter and work with a pastry cutter or 2 knives until crumbly. Stir in just enough cold water (4 to 5 tablespoons) with a fork to make the flour slightly moist and form a rough dough. Divide the dough in half, shape each half into a ball, and flatten slightly. Wrap one ball in plastic wrap and refrigerate for 30 minutes.

With your rolling pin on a lightly floured surface, roll out the remaining dough ball to a 12-inch round. Fit into a 9-inch glass pie dish. Fold the overhanging dough under and crimp decoratively. Chill in the refrigerator for 15 minutes. If you're using Pillsbury dough, which comes as two rolled-up rounds of dough in a box, each in a separate sleeve, roll out one round and place in a 9-inch glass pie dish.

Line the pie shell with foil, fill with dried beans or pie weights, and bake until the sides are set, about 12 minutes. Remove the foil and beans. Reduce the oven temperature to 350°F.

For the filling, scoop out the pulp from the cooled, roasted pumpkin and puree in a food processor until smooth. Add the condensed milk, cream, eggs, cornstarch, molasses, canola oil, cinnamon, ginger, and salt and puree until smooth.

Pour the filling into the pie shell. Bake until the filling is set in the center, about 1 hour. Transfer the pie to a rack and cool for 30 minutes. Serve at room temperature or chilled.

WINTER

Chapter 4

"HUMOR KEEPS US ALIVE. HUMOR AND
FOOD. DON'T FORGET FOOD. YOU CAN
GO A WEEK WITHOUT LAUGHING."
—JOSS WHEDON

WINTER RECIPES

Winter is a slower time of year, one for making memories with
your family. Christmas cookies and fruitcakes fill the air with the seasonal fragrances of cloves, cinnamon, and ginger. In our farmhouse, we always have eggnog made with eggs and cream that we spike with rum or bourbon (non-spiked for my grandkids, of course!). Sometimes, for a really frothy cup, we add ice cream.

I have the fondest memories of making gingerbread houses with Grammy Carl at Christmastime. We would make homemade gingerbread, rolling it out and baking it for a long time at a very low temperature. Our icing was the glue, made simply with confectioners' sugar, egg whites, a little water, and almond or vanilla extract. We'd glue tons of gumdrops all over the house (rooftop shingles) and make a stone walkway leading to the front door with Necco wafers. I looked forward to that special time with Grammy all year.

As we had our fun in the kitchen, my father headed outside and trudged through snow, sleet, and ice in zero-degree temperatures to get to the barn. He fed and milked the cows, cleaned the barn, and washed the milk tank. Farmers are a tenacious brood, filled with dedication.

Nowadays, I string popcorn and cranberries with my grandchildren and wrap them around the Christmas tree during the holidays. It's a very simple, old-fashioned tradition created long before manufactured tinsel and garland.

All of the savory and sweet recipes in this section will make wonderful additions to your holiday spread. And as the New Year brings relief from all the holiday festivities and a longing for an early spring, you can make these comforting, hearty winter meals for your family to cozy up with until the cold spell ends.

FRESH IS AS FRESH AS FROZEN IN
THE NORTHEAST WINTER.

Breakfast Spaghetti Pie

SERVES 4 TO 6

8 ounces spaghetti

4 slices bacon, chopped

1 tablespoon extra-virgin olive oil

1 small onion, thinly sliced

8 large eggs

¼ cup milk

½ cup grated Parmesan cheese

Kosher salt

Freshly ground black pepper

1 cup (4 ounces) shredded mozzarella cheese

½ cup frozen peas, thawed

½ cup cottage cheese

I can't emphasize enough the importance of breakfast, especially for kids. It nourishes their growing brains and keeps their bodies moving! This spaghetti pie will excite the children and get them to eat breakfast. This is also a great rule for leftover pasta; you'll need about 2 cups cooked spaghetti if using leftovers. You could make the pie along with your pasta dinner, or cook it the next morning. If you cooked it with dinner and want to warm it up the next morning, preheat the oven to 350°F and heat the pie for 20 minutes.

PREHEAT THE OVEN to 425°F. Bring a large pot of salted water to a boil. Break the spaghetti into pieces, add to the water, and cook according to the package directions. Drain well.

In a 10-inch ovenproof nonstick skillet over medium heat, cook the bacon in the olive oil until crisp, about 4 minutes. Transfer to a paper towel–lined plate to drain. (If

there's more than 3 tablespoons fat in the pan, pour a little off.) Add the onion to the fat in the pan and cook, stirring occasionally, until light gold and softened, about 7 minutes.

Meanwhile, in a large bowl, whisk together the eggs, milk, and ¼ cup of the Parmesan. Season with salt and pepper and stir in the mozzarella.

When the onion has softened, add the spaghetti, bacon, and peas to the skillet and toss with tongs to coat the spaghetti with the oil. Reduce the heat to medium low and pour in the egg mixture. Once the eggs have just begun to set at the edges, about 5 minutes, dollop the cottage cheese on top in tablespoons. Sprinkle the remaining ¼ cup Parmesan over the top. Transfer the skillet to the oven and bake until the eggs are set in the center and the top is puffy and golden brown, about 20 minutes. Slide the spaghetti pie onto a cutting board and let it rest for 5 minutes before cutting into wedges to serve. The spaghetti pie is also tasty at room temperature. If the kids really balk, offer maple syrup. No, you do not have to eat it with maple syrup—it's all about the kids!

Quinoa Salad

SERVES 4 TO 6

2 teaspoons ground cumin

1 teaspoon paprika

¼ teaspoon cayenne

Kosher salt

Freshly ground black pepper

2 (8-ounce) boneless, skinless chicken breasts, halved and pounded to an even ½-inch thickness (to make 4 thin cutlets)

6 tablespoons extra-virgin olive oil

1 cup quinoa

Grated zest and juice of 1 lemon

1 medium shallot or ½ small red onion, finely chopped (about ¼ cup)

½ cup slivered almonds, toasted

½ cup dried cranberries

¼ cup chopped fresh Italian parsley

This salad is nutritious and tasty. If you have it, you can use 3 cups of leftover roasted or poached chicken instead of grilling the chicken cutlets. You can skip the quinoa if you like and use rice instead. Or you can try another hearty grain like farro, or opt to include no carbs at all. You decide—you're the cook!

IN A SMALL bowl, stir together 1 teaspoon of the cumin, ½ teaspoon of the paprika, and the cayenne with ½ teaspoon kosher salt and a generous grinding of black pepper. Put the chicken on a plate and sprinkle the spices on both sides. Drizzle with 2 tablespoons of the olive oil and rub it in all over the chicken. Let it marinate while you cook the quinoa.

Put the quinoa in a fine strainer, rinse very well under cold water, and drain. Heat a medium saucepan over medium heat and add 1 tablespoon of the olive oil and the quinoa. Cook and stir until the quinoa has dried out, about 3 minutes. Stir in the remaining 1 teaspoon cumin and ½ teaspoon paprika along with ½ teaspoon salt. Add 1¾ cups water, bring to a simmer, and cover. Simmer for 15 minutes. Remove from the heat and let stand for 5 minutes. Fluff with a fork.

Preheat a grill pan to medium high. When the grill is hot, add the chicken and cook, turning once, until just cooked through, 3 to 4 minutes. Let rest on a cutting board for 5 minutes, then chop into bite-size pieces.

In a large bowl, combine the quinoa, chicken, lemon zest and juice, shallot, almonds, cranberries, and parsley. Drizzle with the remaining 3 tablespoons olive oil, toss, and serve. (This can also be made a few hours ahead and refrigerated; just let it come to room temperature again before serving.)

Katherine's Crustless Broccoli, Ham, and Gruyère Quiche

SERVES 6

1 tablespoon unsalted butter, softened

3 cups broccoli florets

4 ounces leftover baked ham, cubed;
or 4 slices crisp crumbled bacon

½ cup chopped scallions

1½ cups (6 ounces) shredded Gruyère cheese

¼ cup grated Parmesan cheese

4 large eggs

2 cups half-and-half

1 tablespoon all-purpose flour

Pinch freshly grated nutmeg

Kosher salt

Freshly ground black pepper

Well, we all have a kitchen mishap tale, and here's mine: I invited Katherine Alford, a culinary queen at Food Network, over for lunch one day and decided to make a quiche that I've made at least 100 times before (and I'm probably hugely underestimating that number). At any rate, I made the quiche the night before so I wouldn't be preoccupied on the morning that I was hosting my important guest. Wrong decision! I heated the quiche in the oven to take the chill off and forgot to take it out. I had to serve Katherine soggy quiche. Not my best moment! Thank goodness I had made two desserts and Katherine has a sweet tooth! Fortunately the quiche still tasted very good, so she insisted that I put the recipe in this cookbook. Here it is. Don't reheat it!

PREHEAT THE OVEN to 350°F. Coat a 9-inch deep-dish pie plate with the softened butter.

Bring a medium saucepan of salted water to a boil. Add the broccoli and boil until crisp-tender, about 3 minutes. Drain, pat very dry, and coarsely chop. Spread the broccoli in the pie plate. Sprinkle the ham and scallions on top, then sprinkle the Gruyère and Parmesan on top of that.

In a large bowl, whisk together the eggs, half-and-half, flour, and nutmeg until smooth. Season with salt and pepper. Pour over the filling in the pie plate. Put the quiche in the center of the middle rack and bake for 50 to 60 minutes, until set. Cool at least 15 minutes before slicing to serve warm or serve at room temperature.

Best Beet Salad

SERVES 4

3 medium beets, washed and trimmed

¼ cup extra-virgin olive oil

2 tablespoons sherry vinegar

1 tablespoon honey

1 tablespoon minced red onion

½ teaspoon Dijon mustard

Kosher salt

Freshly ground black pepper

6 cups baby spinach

½ cup crumbled goat cheese

½ cup coarsely chopped toasted walnuts

Beets are my husband David's other favorite vegetable. And one that he does not get enough of, unlike Brussels sprouts! This salad is simple and delicious.

PREHEAT THE OVEN to 400°F. Wrap the beets individually in tin foil and roast directly on the rack in the oven until tender, about 1 hour. Open the foil packets and let cool. Once they're cool, peel the beets and cut into small chunks.

In a large bowl, whisk together the olive oil, vinegar, honey, red onion, and mustard. Season with salt and pepper. Add the beets and spinach to the dressing and toss to coat. Transfer the salad to a platter or plates, top with the goat cheese and walnuts, and serve.

"THE ONLY REAL STUMBLING BLOCK IS FEAR OF FAILURE. IN COOKING YOU'VE GOT TO HAVE A WHAT-THE-HELL ATTITUDE."
—JULIA CHILD

Splendid Stuffed Mushrooms

SERVES 6

½ cup walnut pieces

24 large white stuffing mushrooms

4 tablespoons unsalted butter

8 ounces sweet Italian sausage, removed from casings

2 cloves garlic, finely chopped

1 cup chopped scallions

½ cup dried breadcrumbs

½ cup shredded Gruyère cheese

½ cup grated Parmesan cheese

¼ cup chopped fresh Italian parsley

Kosher salt

Freshly ground black pepper

Years ago, I met a dear friend named Bud (Sydney) Tudge, a former chef at the Waldorf Astoria who found his way to the Hudson Valley. Bud opened a clam stand in a little town and served the best fried clams and coleslaw to ever come down the pike. His clam stand eventually evolved into a full restaurant, which sadly closed after he died. He was a mentor to me for years and it was he who insisted that these stuffed mushrooms would be a boon to my very newly established catering company. He was correct.

PREHEAT THE OVEN to 375°F. Place the walnuts on a baking sheet and toast in the oven until golden and fragrant, about 5 minutes. Cool, finely chop, and set aside.

Wash the mushrooms with a damp cloth and remove the stems and the dark-colored gills inside if the mushrooms are older. Finely chop the stems. If the mushroom caps are very round, trim a small slice off the tops so they will sit level on the baking sheet.

In a large skillet over medium heat, melt 2 tablespoons of the butter. Add the sausage and cook and crumble into small pieces with a wooden spoon until no longer pink, about 4 minutes. Add the chopped mushroom stems and cook until tender and no liquid remains in the pan (increase the heat if needed to boil away the excess water that the mushrooms give off), about 6 minutes. Add the garlic and cook until fragrant, about 1 minute. Scrape the mixture into a bowl and let cool completely.

Add the chopped walnuts, scallions, breadcrumbs, Gruyère, Parmesan, and parsley to the sausage mixture and season with salt and pepper. In a large bowl, toss the mushroom caps with the remaining 2 tablespoons butter and season with salt. Stuff the mushrooms with the filling, dividing it evenly. Arrange the stuffed mushrooms on a rimmed baking sheet and bake until the caps are tender and the filling is crispy, 17 to 18 minutes.

Gracious Grapes

SERVES 10 AS AN HORS D'OEUVRE

1½ pounds seedless red or green grapes, or a combination

2 cups toasted walnut pieces

¼ cup chopped fresh Italian parsley

8 ounces block cream cheese, softened

4 ounces Roquefort or other crumbly blue cheese

4 to 5 tablespoons heavy cream

This supersimple hors d'oeuvre or starter was a favorite with my catering clients. The grapes look very delicate and pretty, especially when garnished with a bouquet of parsley and served on a glass plate. The only trick is to make sure the grapes are very dry so the cream cheese mixture sticks. If you're making this for a smaller group, you can easily cut the recipe in half—or make them all, they will keep for several days in the fridge and make a great snack too!

REMOVE THE GRAPES from the stems (you should have about 4 cups). Wash and dry the grapes very well. Roll them on a rimmed baking sheet lined with a kitchen towel to dry completely.

Finely chop the walnuts by hand; you want them finely chopped, but not pasty. Put the chopped nuts in a shallow bowl, stir in the parsley, and set aside. With a handheld mixer, mix the cream cheese and Roquefort in a medium bowl until smooth. Add the heavy cream, a tablespoon at a time, until the mixture is the consistency of softened butter.

Roll the grapes in the cream cheese mixture a handful at a time until they are completely coated, then roll in the nuts. (It's easiest to roll them in the cheese using a fork or spoon to keep your hands clean for rolling in the nuts.) Rest on a parchment-lined baking sheet while you roll the remaining grapes. Chill the grapes until the cheese is firm, about 1 hour.

Pizza Party Dip

SERVES 8

1 large oblong loaf Italian bread

8 ounces block cream cheese, softened

¼ cup mayonnaise

½ cup grated Parmesan cheese

1 teaspoon dried oregano

¼ teaspoon granulated garlic

Kosher salt

Freshly ground black pepper

1 cup prepared pizza sauce

1 cup (4 ounces) shredded mozzarella cheese

Pizza toppings of your choice: I like pepperoni, chopped bell pepper, and olives

Fresh basil leaves

Breadsticks, for serving

This is a great dip for serving at a football party or to a crowd at an informal gathering. It's tasty and easy to eat standing up. Start people off with breadsticks and bread chunks for dipping, then encourage them to tear off pieces of the dip-soaked bowl to finish!

PREHEAT THE OVEN to 400°F. With a serrated knife, cut an inch or so from the top of the bread to make a flat surface. Cut the top crosswise into slices. Cut or tear out the center of the bread in large chunks to make a bowl; cut the chunks into cubes, for dipping later. Spread the bread cubes on a baking sheet and toast in the oven just until crisp, 5 to 7 minutes. Set aside.

In a food processor, combine the cream cheese, mayonnaise, ¼ cup of the Parmesan, the oregano, and granulated garlic and pulse until smooth. Season with salt and pepper. Spread in the bottom of the bread bowl.

Spread the pizza sauce over the cream cheese, then sprinkle with the mozzarella and remaining ¼ cup Parmesan. Top with the pizza toppings of your choice. Put the bread bowl on a baking sheet and bake until the dip is heated through and bubbly, 15 to 20 minutes. Tear some fresh basil leaves over the top and serve with the toasted bread and breadsticks.

Cold Day
Corn Chowder

SERVES 6

2 tablespoons unsalted butter

4 thick slices bacon, chopped

1 medium onion, finely chopped

1 small red bell pepper, finely chopped

2 stalks celery, finely chopped

Kosher salt

Freshly ground black pepper

3 tablespoons all-purpose flour

1 tablespoon chopped fresh thyme

1 teaspoon paprika

2 bay leaves

6 cups low-sodium chicken broth

1 large russet potato (about 12 ounces), peeled and cut into ½-inch chunks

1 cup half-and-half or heavy cream

3 to 4 cups frozen fresh corn kernels (from 6 ears fresh corn) or 8-ounce store-bought packages frozen corn, thawed and drained

Chopped fresh chives or parsley for garnish

My neighbors in the Hudson Valley who own Holmquest Farms, Terry and Tom, love this soup. But Tom always eats it before Terry can get to it.

Though it is optional, pureeing a little of the soup and adding it back in adds creaminess and makes the soup taste "cornier" because it distributes the corn flavor throughout.

I shuck and freeze fresh corn in the summer. Shuck the corn and cut the kernels from the cob by holding the corn vertically in a bowl and shaving off the kernels with a sharp knife. You should get 3 to 4 cups of corn kernels from 6 ears, depending on the size of the ears. Freeze in plastic bags.

IN A MEDIUM Dutch oven, melt the butter over medium heat. Add the bacon and cook, stirring occasionally, until crisp. Transfer to paper towels to drain.

Drain or spoon off all but 3 tablespoons of the fat in the pot. Add the onion, bell pepper, and celery and cook, stirring occasionally, until the vegetables just begin to become tender, about 5 minutes. Season with salt and pepper and add the flour, thyme, paprika, and bay leaves. Stir the flour into the vegetables to make a paste and coat them evenly. Cook a minute or two to get rid of the raw flour smell. Add the chicken broth and bring to a simmer. Cover and simmer until all of the vegetables are tender, about 15 minutes.

Uncover the pot and add the potato, half-and-half, and corn. Simmer, uncovered, until the potato is very tender but not yet falling apart, 10 to 12 minutes. If desired, puree about a cup of the soup in a food processor or blender and stir it back into the soup. Discard the bay leaves. Serve garnished with the cooked bacon and some chives or parsley.

...centuries been

...come another day on which to spy into the
...century maiden loves mystery, she
...as the flames will divulge her fate on Candlemas.
congenial party of six or eight, ten at the outside, with a
...depends upon the guests, and the most enjoyable affairs are
always small and informal.

The table centerpiece should be of dainty, white flowers,
Roman hyacinths, lilies of the valley, carnations, or lilies

...used. These may be
...ice cream frozen in the shape of c
...for wicks, which are lighted just
...wax matches with which each gue
If a flame flickers without a visibl
...windy; if the candle is slow to light
the first candle to go out foretells a
one to burn the longest signifies w
candles are entirely burned out let each
steps away, then see if the flame can
puff, for each puff adds one year's delay

A Dickens Party

On February the seventh, in the year r
Charles Dickens was born, so let us rem

9

"Mother's" Pasta, Beans, and Greens Soup

SERVES 6 PLUS LEFTOVERS

¼ cup extra-virgin olive oil

2 cups diced ham (from a leftover ham, like Tavern Ham, page 47)

2 medium leeks, white and light green parts, halved and sliced (about 2 cups)

2 medium carrots, chopped (about 2 cups)

2 stalks celery, chopped (about 1 cup)

¼ cup tomato paste

3 cloves garlic, chopped

1 tablespoon chopped fresh thyme

1½ quarts low-sodium chicken broth

2 bay leaves

Kosher salt

Freshly ground black pepper

½ small head savoy cabbage, shredded (about 6 cups)

1 large head escarole (or other hearty green such as kale), coarsely shredded (about 8 cups)

1 (15-ounce) can cannellini or other white beans, rinsed and drained

1 cup ditalini or other small pasta shape

Grated Parmesan cheese, for serving

Rosella Shader, my sister-in-law Beverly's mother, whom I call Mother, is the inspiration for this soup. I named it after her because she's very dear to me and has all the qualities of my grandmothers, and also because she loved eating this soup when she traveled through Italy last year. Rosella, also known as Elenore, is 80 years old, but she looks and acts more like a 50-year-old and can cook circles around anyone I know. I am blessed to have her in my life.

You can leave the ham out for a slightly lighter but still delicious vegetarian soup. Use vegetable broth in place of chicken broth.

THE SIGN OF A GOOD COOK IS THE RESULT OF GOOD SOUP.

HEAT A LARGE Dutch oven over medium heat and add the olive oil. When the oil is hot, add the ham and cook and stir until browned, about 4 minutes. Lower the heat to medium and add the leeks, carrots, and celery. Cook, stirring occasionally, until the leeks are wilted, about 8 minutes. Clear a space in the pan and add the tomato paste. Let it toast for a minute, then add the garlic and thyme and stir it all into the vegetables. Add the chicken broth, 2 quarts water, and the bay leaves. Season with salt and pepper, remembering that the ham and broth are already salted. Bring to a simmer, cover, and cook for 30 minutes to let the flavors develop.

Add the cabbage, escarole, and beans and bring the soup to a rapid simmer to reduce it while the vegetables cook. Simmer until the cabbage and escarole are very tender, 30 to 40 minutes.

If the soup is too thick at this point, add up to 1 cup water. Add the pasta and cook until just tender (it will cook more when the soup is off the heat too), about 5 minutes. Discard the bay leaves. Serve the soup in big bowls with grated Parmesan sprinkled on top.

Many-Mushroom Soup
with Cheesy Toasts

SERVES 6 PLUS LEFTOVERS

MUSHROOM SOUP

½ cup dried mushrooms

1 cup boiling water

¼ cup extra-virgin olive oil

2 pounds mixed fresh mushrooms
(use a combination of white, cremini,
shiitake, oyster, chanterelle, morel,
even porcini if you want to go all out),
thickly sliced

Kosher salt

Freshly ground black pepper

3 medium leeks, white and light
green parts, halved and sliced

2 stalks celery, chopped

1 medium carrot, chopped

2 cloves garlic, finely chopped

1 tablespoon chopped fresh thyme

3 tablespoons tomato paste

1½ teaspoons sweet or smoked paprika
(either is nice; smoked paprika will give
a little heartier flavor to the soup)

2½ quarts low-sodium chicken broth

2 teaspoons Worcestershire sauce

2 bay leaves

½ cup pearled barley

¼ cup chopped fresh Italian parsley

CHEESY TOASTS

1 small baguette

Extra-virgin olive oil, for brushing

½ cup finely shredded Cheddar cheese

½ cup grated Parmesan cheese

2 tablespoons chopped fresh Italian parsley

Dried mushrooms are the secret weapon here. Soaking them adds an extra step, but it's definitely worth it to take this soup to the next level, flavor-wise. Just half a cup imparts a deep mushroom flavor to a whole pot of soup. Most grocery stores sell them in little bags and they're not very expensive, unless you are buying porcini.

FOR THE SOUP, put the dried mushrooms in a spouted measuring cup and add 1 cup boiling water. Let the mushrooms soak for 10 minutes, until softened. Drain, reserving the soaking liquid, and finely chop the mushrooms.

In a large Dutch oven over medium-high heat, add the olive oil. When the oil is hot, add half of the fresh mushrooms and let them sit in the pan until the undersides begin to brown and sizzle, about 2 minutes. Stir and brown the other sides, about 2 minutes more. Don't stir too much or the mushrooms will steam instead of brown. Add the remaining mushrooms and brown those too, about 4 more minutes. Season with salt and pepper.

Reduce the heat to medium and add the leeks, celery, carrot, garlic, and thyme. Cook, stirring occasionally, until the leeks are wilted but not browned, about 8 minutes. Clear a little space in the middle of the pan with your spoon and drop in the tomato paste. Let it sit and toast in that spot for a minute or two, sprinkle with the paprika, then stir into the vegetables. Add the chicken broth, Worcestershire sauce, and bay leaves. Stir in the reconstituted dried mushrooms. Pour in their soaking liquid, leaving any grit at the bottom in the measuring cup. Bring the soup to a simmer. Simmer, uncovered, until the mushrooms are tender, about 20 minutes.

Uncover, add the barley, and cook until the barley is just tender, about 35 minutes. In the last few minutes, turn up the heat to reduce and thicken the soup to your liking.

Meanwhile, make the cheesy toasts. Preheat the oven to 400°F. Slice the baguette into ½-inch-thick slices on a slight bias (you'll get about 12 slices), and arrange on a baking sheet. Bake until just toasted, not too golden, about 5 minutes. Remove the toasts from the oven and brush the tops with olive oil. Switch the oven to broil. In a small bowl, toss together the Cheddar and the Parmesan. Sprinkle the cheese on the toasts and broil until the cheese is just melted and bubbly, 45 seconds to 1 minute. Transfer to a plate or platter and sprinkle with the parsley.

Remove the bay leaves from the soup and discard. Place the soup in a tureen or service pot or ladle into a bowl. Sprinkle with fresh chopped parsley and serve with cheesy toasts.

Perfect Mashed Potatoes

SERVES 8 PLUS LEFTOVERS

4 pounds russet potatoes, whole

Kosher salt

3 cloves garlic, smashed and peeled

½ cup (1 stick) unsalted butter

1 cup half-and-half, plus more as needed

½ cup sour cream

Freshly grated black pepper

This rule makes a big bowl of potatoes for a holiday gathering or meal for the whole family. This was a Grammy Tabor favorite, and my mom's as well. Grammy Carl made the most delicious creamed potatoes, but that's for another day!

With this recipe, you'll have enough leftovers for potato patties fried in butter the next day. All you do is take a scoop of cold mashed potatoes, make a patty, and fry it in butter. Yum!

PUT THE POTATOES in a large saucepan with salted water to cover and drop in the garlic. Bring to a simmer and cook until the potatoes are tender when pierced with a fork but *not* falling apart, 30 to 35 minutes. Drain, and when the potatoes are cool enough to handle, peel them. Reserve the cooked garlic.

In the pot used to cook the potatoes, melt the butter in the half-and-half over low heat. Add the warm peeled potatoes, reserved garlic, and sour cream. Mash with a masher until the potatoes are as smooth as you like, adding up to a ¼ cup more half-and-half if they seem dry. Season with salt and pepper and serve.

Creamy Cauliflower Mash

SERVES 6 TO 8

2 small heads cauliflower
(about 2½ pounds total)

Kosher salt

4 cloves garlic, smashed and peeled

4 tablespoons cream cheese, softened

4 tablespoons unsalted butter

Freshly ground black pepper

1 cup grated Parmesan cheese

This mash is a lovely alternative to mashed potatoes—some people can't even tell the difference. For a smaller gathering or a weeknight dinner side dish, use just one head of cauliflower and halve the rest of the recipe. This can also be made ahead for a holiday meal: Spread the cauliflower mash in a buttered casserole dish, sprinkle with a little more cheese, and cover with foil. Bake in a 400°F oven until heated through, then uncover and bake just to brown the top. You can also mash this straight in the pot, but the extra step in the food processor makes a delicious, creamy mash.

CUT THE CAULIFLOWER into florets of 1 or 2 inches. Discard the tough leaves and core, but you can, and should, include the tender leaves closest to the cauliflower. Bring 2 cups water to a simmer in a large saucepan. Season the water with salt and drop in the garlic. Add the cauliflower, adjust the heat so the water is just simmering, and cover the pot. Cook until the cauliflower is *very* tender, about 15 minutes.

Drain the cauliflower, reserving a little of the cooking water. Add the hot cauliflower, cream cheese, garlic, and butter to a food processor (you may need to do this in batches, which is fine, just divide the cream cheese and the butter between the batches). Season with salt and pepper. Pulse a few times to melt the butter and cream cheese. Then puree until very smooth, adding just a little cooking water if it seems too thick or isn't pureeing properly.

Transfer the cauliflower mash to a serving bowl, stir in the Parmesan, and serve hot.

"COOKING IS AT ONCE CHILD'S PLAY AND ADULT JOY.
AND COOKING DONE WITH CARE IS AN ACT OF LOVE."
—CRAIG CLAIBORNE

Tomato Soup

SERVES 6

3 tablespoons unsalted butter

2 medium leeks, white and light green parts, thinly sliced

1 medium carrot, shredded

2 cloves garlic, smashed and peeled

1 tablespoon chopped fresh thyme

Kosher salt

Freshly ground black pepper

1 (28-ounce) can whole tomatoes, crushed by hand

2 tablespoons tomato paste

1 teaspoon sugar, or to taste

3 cups low-sodium chicken broth

2 bay leaves

1 cup heavy cream

Crème fraîche or sour cream, for garnish

Chopped fresh dill, for garnish

Tomato soup was my daughter Kimberlee's favorite soup when she was a child. She always preferred vegetables to meat.

In my version of the classic soup, I use leeks because I think they create a smoother flavor with the tomatoes. The amount of sugar you'll use will really depend on the quality of your canned tomatoes, so start with 1 teaspoon and then taste again after the soup has simmered a few minutes. Err on the side of less is more; the sugar is in the recipe only to cut the acid from the tomatoes! I serve the soup with a little dill sprinkled on top, which adds a hint of freshness to both the taste and the presentation.

IN A LARGE saucepan, melt the butter over medium heat. Add the leeks, carrot, garlic, and thyme and season with salt and pepper. Cook, stirring occasionally, until the leeks are softened, about 6 minutes. Add the canned tomatoes, tomato paste, and sugar. Bring to a simmer, then add the broth and bay leaves. Season with salt and pepper and simmer until all of the vegetables are very tender, 15 to 20 minutes. Taste, and add more sugar if needed.

Discard the bay leaves, add the cream, and simmer for 5 more minutes, then remove from the heat. Puree in a blender (in batches, be careful!) or right in the pot with a handheld immersion blender until smooth. Reheat the soup over low heat. Serve with a dollop of crème fraîche and chopped dill.

Easy and Cheesy

SERVES 6 TO 8

Unsalted butter, softened,
for the baking dish

8 to 10 thick slices day-old country
white bread (about ½ inch thick, cut
from a long square Pullman loaf)

1 bunch asparagus (about 1 pound)

6 large eggs

2½ cups whole milk

1 cup heavy cream

1 bunch scallions, chopped (about 1 cup)

2 tablespoons chopped fresh
Italian parsley

¼ teaspoon freshly grated nutmeg

Kosher salt

Freshly ground black pepper

8 ounces mild Swiss cheese, shredded

½ cup grated Parmesan cheese

We all need a little more time in our busy lives.
The beauty of this casserole is that it can be
made several hours ahead (or even better, the
night before), so all you have to do is pop it in
the oven when people start arriving. The other
great thing about this casserole is that you won't
have to clear any space in your refrigerator for
leftovers—it's that good!

PREHEAT THE OVEN to 400°F. Grease a shallow
3-quart casserole dish with the softened butter. Bring
a large pot of salted water to a boil.

Cut or tear the bread into bite-size chunks (or cut each
slice of bread into 4 squares). Arrange the bread on a
baking sheet and toast in the oven until the bread dries
a bit but hasn't taken on any color, about 8 minutes.

Meanwhile, break off the woody ends of the asparagus
and discard. Peel the bottom half of the stalks (if you

want) and cut the asparagus into 2-inch pieces. Drop into
the boiling water and cook until bright green and crisp-
tender, about 3 minutes. Drain under cold running water
and pat very dry.

In a large bowl, whisk together the eggs, milk, cream,
scallions, parsley, and nutmeg and season with salt and
pepper. Layer half of the bread in the bottom of the
buttered casserole. Arrange the asparagus on top and
sprinkle with half of the Swiss and Parmesan. Layer
the remaining bread on top and pour the custard over.
Sprinkle the top with the remaining Swiss and
Parmesan. Refrigerate for at least 1 hour so the bread
soaks up the custard (overnight is even better).

Remove the casserole from the fridge and let sit at
room temperature while you preheat the oven to
350°F. Bake until the casserole is cooked through and
the top is puffed and golden, about 45 minutes.

"THE CONSCIOUS WATER SAW ITS GOD AND BLUSHED."
—RICHARD CRASHAW

Beloved Beef Wellington

SERVES 6

1 (2-pound) center-cut beef tenderloin, tied by your butcher

Kosher salt

Freshly ground black pepper

3 tablespoons extra-virgin olive oil

2 tablespoons Dijon mustard

1½ tablespoons prepared horseradish, drained

1 pound button mushrooms

4 tablespoons unsalted butter

1 shallot, minced

2 tablespoons heavy cream

2 tablespoons dried breadcrumbs

2 tablespoons finely chopped fresh Italian parsley

1 large egg

All-purpose flour, for dusting

1 sheet frozen puff pastry (from a 17.3-ounce package), thawed in the refrigerator

Flaky sea salt, for sprinkling

My best friend Betsy loves my beef Wellington. Not only is it delicious, but it is also a show-stopper in the presentation department. Just slice into the golden pastry to reveal the rosy-red beef roast inside and serve on a platter garnished with some fresh herbs. I can hear Betsy's stomach growling all the way from my farm!

SPRINKLE THE TENDERLOIN generously on all sides with salt and pepper. Heat 2 tablespoons of the oil in a large skillet over high heat. Sear the beef on all sides, 8 to 10 minutes. Transfer to a baking sheet and let the beef cool completely, about 20 minutes.

Once the beef is cool to the touch, snip off the butcher's twine and discard. Combine the Dijon and horseradish in a small bowl and spread all over the beef. Place in the refrigerator to chill for 1 hour.

Meanwhile, add half of the mushrooms to a food processor and pulse until they are very finely chopped. Transfer to a bowl and repeat with the remaining mushrooms. Melt the butter and remaining 1 table-spoon oil in a large skillet over medium-high heat. Add the shallot and cook until softened, about 4 minutes. Add the mushrooms and cook until they release all their moisture and then dry, about 10 minutes. Add the cream and simmer until thick, about 2 minutes. Turn off the heat and stir in the breadcrumbs and parsley. Transfer the mushrooms to a small bowl, cool completely, then chill in the refrigerator for at least 1 hour. The mushrooms should now look like a paste.

Continued

Preheat the oven to 400°F. Line a baking sheet with parchment paper. Crack the egg into a small bowl and beat until smooth. Dust the work area lightly with flour. Roll out the puff pastry so it's 4 inches longer and 6 to 7 inches wider than the tenderloin. Brush a 3-inch border on the pastry with the beaten egg. Spread and pat half of the mushroom mixture all over the top and sides of the beef. Lay the beef, mushroom side down, in the center of the pastry and pat the remaining mushrooms onto the exposed side. Fold the two ends of the pastry over the beef and then fold up the other sides. Press to seal. Place the beef seam side down on the prepared baking sheet. Brush all over with the egg wash. Cut three slits on the top of the pastry and sprinkle lightly with flaky sea salt.

Roast until a thermometer inserted into the center of the beef reads 120°F, about 40 minutes. Remove from the oven and rest for 20 minutes; the temperature will rise to 125°F, leaving you with a nice ruby-red medium rare. Slice the Wellington into 1-inch-thick pieces and serve.

"IF YOU WANT TO BE SUCCESSFUL, IT'S JUST THIS SIMPLE. KNOW WHAT YOU ARE DOING. LOVE WHAT YOU ARE DOING. AND BELIEVE IN WHAT YOU ARE DOING."
—WILL ROGERS

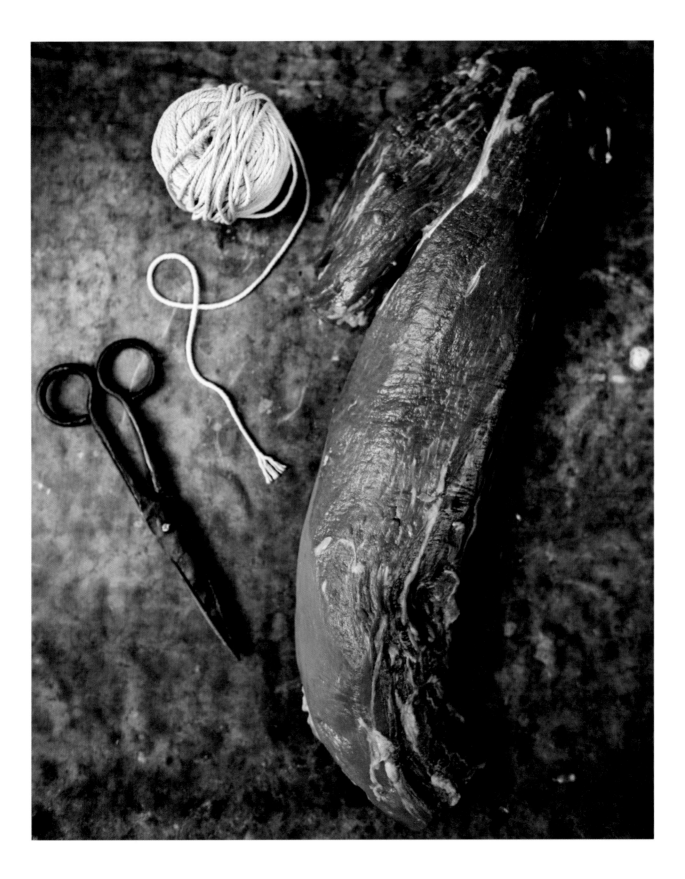

Marvelous Meat Loaf

SERVES 6

1 pound ground beef

1 pound ground pork

2 large eggs

1 cup (8 ounces) finely shredded Cheddar cheese

¼ cup grated Parmesan cheese

¾ cup breadcrumbs

½ cup finely chopped onion

½ cup milk

¼ cup chopped fresh Italian parsley

2 cloves garlic, chopped

½ cup ketchup

2 tablespoons Dijon mustard

Kosher salt

Freshly ground black pepper

Olive oil, for the roasting pan

3 slices bacon, halved crosswise

1 tablespoon light brown sugar

1 tablespoon cider vinegar

This one is not just a farmhouse staple—it's an every house staple! The meatloaf will serve 6, plus maybe some leftovers for sandwiches, depending on how thick you cut your slices. I try to make enough to be certain I have leftovers. Cold meat-loaf sandwiches with onion and mayo—yum!

PREHEAT THE OVEN to 375°F. In a large bowl, combine the ground beef, ground pork, eggs, Cheddar, Parmesan, breadcrumbs, onion, milk, parsley, garlic, ¼ cup of the ketchup, 1 tablespoon of the Dijon, and salt and pepper. Mix with your hands to combine.

Brush a roasting pan with olive oil. Form the meat mixture into a loaf (about 12 inches long) in the roasting pan. Lay the bacon slices over the top. Bake the meat loaf until the bacon is cooked, about 30 minutes.

In a small bowl, stir together the remaining ¼ cup ketchup, remaining 1 tablespoon mustard, the brown sugar, and the vinegar. When the bacon is cooked, brush the meat loaf with half of the glaze. Return the meat loaf to the oven and continue to bake, glazing every 15 minutes, until the internal temperature reads 165°F on an instant-read thermometer, about 45 minutes more. Let the meat loaf rest for 15 minutes before slicing.

Braised Short Ribs

SERVES 4

2 large dried New Mexico chili peppers, stemmed, seeded, and torn into pieces

1 cup boiling water

3 cups low-sodium chicken broth

2 tablespoons tomato paste

1 large onion, chopped

4 cloves garlic, smashed and peeled

Kosher salt

5 pounds meaty English-style center-cut short ribs

Freshly ground black pepper

3 tablespoons extra-virgin olive oil

1 (750-milliliter) bottle hard cider

2 tablespoons balsamic vinegar

3 sprigs fresh rosemary

Chopped fresh Italian parsley, for garnish

This is a great recipe. When I asked my was-band why he married me, he said, "Because you can make short ribs." Well, we all can't be poetic! Ironically, it's also one of my now-husband David's favorite meals.

PREHEAT THE OVEN to 325°F and adjust the rack to the bottom third of the oven. Put the chilies in a medium bowl and pour over the boiling water. Let soak until softened, about 15 minutes.

In a blender, combine the softened peppers, their soaking water, the chicken broth, tomato paste, onion, and garlic. Season with salt. Blend until smooth.

Sprinkle the short ribs generously on both sides with salt and pepper. Heat the olive oil in a large Dutch oven over medium-high heat. In batches, sear the short ribs until browned on all sides, 8 to 10 minutes per batch. Transfer the short ribs to a plate as they brown.

Once all of the ribs are out of the pot, add the cider and bring to a boil, scraping up the brown bits from the bottom of the pot. Pour the blended chili mixture into the pot and bring to a boil. Add the vinegar and rosemary sprigs and boil to reduce slightly, 2 to 3 minutes. Return the short ribs and any juice that may have accumulated on the plate back to the pot. Cover tightly and bake in the oven until very tender, about 2½ hours.

Transfer the ribs to a platter and cover with foil to keep warm. Reduce the sauce in the pot over medium heat until thick and saucy, about 15 minutes. Discard the rosemary stems. Add the ribs back to the pot before serving to coat with the reduced sauce. Place the ribs on plates and ladle the sauce over the top. Sprinkle with chopped parsley and serve.

Spicy Chicken and Chips

SERVES 6 TO 8

....

7 ounces corn tortilla chips
(about half a bag), coarsely crushed

2 tablespoons unsalted butter
(plus more for the baking dish)

1 bunch scallions, chopped (about 1 cup)

2 cloves garlic, chopped

2 tablespoons all-purpose flour

1 tablespoon chili powder

1 teaspoon cumin

½ teaspoon cayenne

1 cup low-sodium chicken broth

1 cup heavy cream

1 (10-ounce) can diced tomatoes and
green chilies (such as Ro-Tel), drained

3½ cups leftover diced chicken

1 (15-ounce) can pinto beans,
rinsed and drained

Kosher salt

2 cups (8 ounces) shredded
Cheddar cheese

Sour cream, for serving

....

When my kids were little, they'd pick the green chilies off their plates. Now that they're adults, they love this recipe.

Leftover chicken works well here, but you can also poach your own chicken breasts, then remove the skin and bone and dice the meat. In place of the broth, make a light stock by reducing the poaching liquid.

PREHEAT THE OVEN to 400°F. Butter a 3-quart oval casserole. Sprinkle a third of the crushed chips in the bottom of the casserole.

In a medium saucepan, melt the butter over medium heat. Add the scallions and garlic and cook until the scallions are wilted, about 3 minutes. Add the flour, chili powder, cumin, and cayenne. Cook and stir until the spices are fragrant, about 1 minute. Whisk in the chicken broth and cream and bring to a simmer. Cook until thickened, about 3 minutes. Pour the sauce into a large bowl. Add the tomatoes and chilies, chicken, and beans and stir to combine. Season with salt.

Spread half of the mixture on top of the chips in the casserole and top with half of the cheese. Layer another third of the chips, then the remaining chicken mixture. In a medium bowl, toss together the remaining chips and cheese, then sprinkle over the top of the casserole. Cover with foil and bake until heated through, about 30 minutes. Uncover and bake until bubbly, 10 to 15 minutes more. Let rest for 10 minutes before serving with sour cream on the side.

Quick Chick
Chunks 'n' Chew Stew

SERVES 6

4 boneless, skinless chicken breasts
(about 2¼ pounds), cut into 1½-inch chunks

Kosher salt

Freshly ground black pepper

1 cup all-purpose flour

2 teaspoons paprika

1 teaspoon granulated garlic

1 teaspoon granulated onion

2 tablespoons unsalted butter

2 tablespoons extra-virgin olive oil

4 medium carrots, cut into 1½-inch chunks

4 medium red potatoes, cut
into 1½-inch chunks

4 stalks celery, cut into 1½-inch chunks

4 small leeks, white and light green parts,
halved and cut into 1½-inch chunks

2 sprigs fresh sage

1 quart low-sodium chicken broth

⅓ cup heavy cream

2 bay leaves

¼ cup chopped fresh Italian parsley

Juice of ½ lemon

Say that three times fast! This is another old family favorite. I served it on biscuits when the kids were young. My mother liked it on toast points. Grammy Tabor served it over mashed potatoes. And Great-Gramma Williams served it with dumplings. It's been around awhile! If you'd like to save some calories, and time, omit the butter and flour and add a bit of heavy cream at the end instead.

PAT THE CHICKEN dry and season with salt and pepper. In a shallow bowl or a rimmed plate, combine the flour, paprika, granulated garlic, and granulated onion. Melt 1 tablespoon of the butter in the olive oil in a large Dutch oven over medium-high heat. Lightly dredge the chicken in the flour. Reserve ¼ cup of the flour. In batches, add the chicken to the pot and cook until browned, 2 to 3 minutes per batch. Transfer the pieces to a plate as they brown.

Once all of the chicken is browned, add the remaining 1 tablespoon butter to the pot, along with the carrots, potatoes, celery, leeks, and sage sprigs. Season with salt and pepper. Cook, stirring occasionally, until the vegetables just begin to brown, about 5 minutes. Sprinkle with the ¼ cup reserved flour and stir to coat the vegetables in the flour. Add the chicken broth, cream, and bay leaves. Bring to a simmer, cover, and cook until the vegetables are just tender, about 20 minutes.

Return the chicken to the pot along with the parsley and simmer until the chicken is cooked through, about 5 minutes more. Discard the bay leaves and sage sprigs. Stir in the lemon juice, adjust the seasoning, and serve.

Chop-Chop-in-the-Pot
Pork Chops

SERVES 4

½ cup all-purpose flour

1 teaspoon granulated garlic

1 teaspoon granulated onion

1 teaspoon paprika

¼ teaspoon cayenne

4 boneless pork loin chops
(about 1¾ pounds and 1 inch thick)

Kosher salt

3 tablespoons unsalted butter

2 tablespoons chopped fresh thyme

1 cup low-sodium chicken broth

½ cup heavy cream

1 tablespoon Dijon mustard

2 tablespoons chopped fresh
Italian parsley

Pork chops were my daughter Lorinda's favorite when she was young. Since she was an avid reader, I always knew when she liked a certain dish because she wouldn't excuse herself from the table immediately to go and read. The reading served her well, however. She is words away from her PhD. Congratulations, Ree!

Be careful not to overcook the chops. It's all about the moisture when you're cooking pork.

IN A GALLON-SIZE resealable plastic bag, combine the flour, granulated garlic, granulated onion, paprika, and cayenne. Shake to mix. Season the pork chops with salt, add to the bag, and shake to coat in the seasoned flour. Remove the chops. Reserve 3 tablespoons of the seasoned flour.

Melt 2 tablespoons of the butter in a large skillet over medium heat. Add the coated pork chops and brown on both sides, about 2 minutes per side. Remove the chops to a plate.

Add the remaining 1 tablespoon butter and the thyme to the skillet. Sprinkle the reserved 3 tablespoons seasoned flour over the fat left in the pan. Cook, stirring to scrape up the browned bits, until the flour is light gold, about 2 minutes. Add the chicken broth and cream and bring to a simmer. Nestle the pork chops back in the pan and simmer until the sauce is thick and the pork chops are cooked through, 6 to 8 minutes. Stir the mustard and parsley into the sauce and serve.

Exceptional
Veal Marsala

SERVES 4

All-purpose flour, for dredging

1¼ pounds veal leg cutlets, pounded to an even ¼-inch thickness (by you or your butcher)

Kosher salt

Freshly ground black pepper

3 tablespoons extra-virgin olive oil

3 tablespoons unsalted butter

1½ pounds mixed mushrooms (button, cremini, shiitake, chanterelle, oyster, etc.), sliced

2 shallots, finely chopped (about ½ cup)

2 teaspoons chopped fresh thyme

½ cup dry Marsala

1½ cups low-sodium chicken broth

2 tablespoons chopped fresh Italian parsley

A little goes a long way in this recipe since the veal is sliced so thin. A little more than a pound of veal will easily feed 4. Veal cutlets that are on sale at the grocery store are usually cut from the leg, and they take a bit of cooking time to become tender. If you want to splurge, get pounded cutlets from the rib or loin; they're pricier but are very tender and will cook in just a few minutes per side, then need only a quick dip into the sauce at the end.

David and I enjoy this dish served with orzo, David's favorite pasta. A green salad lightly dressed is all you need to round out the meal.

SPREAD THE FLOUR on a plate. Season the cutlets with salt and pepper and lightly dredge on both sides in the flour, tapping off the excess.

Heat a large skillet over medium-high heat and add half of the olive oil. When the oil is hot, add half of the cutlets and brown both sides, about 1 minute per side. Transfer to a plate and use the remaining olive oil to brown the remaining cutlets.

When all of the cutlets are browned, return the skillet to medium-high heat and add the butter. Add half of the mushrooms and cook, without stirring, until browned on the undersides, about 3 minutes. Add the remaining mushrooms and stir and brown again, about 4 minutes more. Reduce the heat to medium and add the shallots and thyme. Cook until the shallots are wilted, about 4 minutes.

Add the Marsala, bring to a boil, and cook until reduced by half and syrupy, about 2 minutes. Add the chicken broth and return to a simmer. Nestle the cutlets in the sauce and simmer until tender (you should be able to easily cut through the edge of one with a knife), about 30 minutes. Season the sauce with salt and pepper, stir in the parsley, and serve.

Upriver Salmon

SERVES 4

Extra-virgin olive oil, for brushing the baking dish

1 side of salmon, 2 to 3 pounds, flesh side up

½ teaspoon granulated garlic

½ teaspoon granulated onion

Kosher salt

Freshly ground black pepper

2 tablespoons Dijon mustard

2 tablespoons mayonnaise

Grated zest and juice of ½ lemon

2 tablespoons chopped fresh Italian parsley, plus more for garnish

1 tablespoon chopped fresh dill, plus more for garnish

When David and I took a cruise to Alaska with a group of colleagues and friends, my most vivid memory was watching the salmon swim upriver. The other nifty experience was fishing for salmon in the Alaskan waters, *and* catching them! And then we had them frozen and sent home, which extended our experience for many weeks thereafter.

If you want leftovers for the Salmon Salad Sandwiches (page 10), buy another side of salmon and double the basting sauce. If you don't like dill, you could use tarragon, chervil, or just parsley instead.

PREHEAT THE OVEN to 425°F. Brush a 9- by 13-inch glass or ceramic baking dish with olive oil. Season the salmon with the granulated garlic, granulated onion, and some salt and pepper.

In a small bowl, mix together the Dijon, mayonnaise, lemon zest and juice, parsley, and dill. Put the salmon in the oiled pan, skin side down, and brush with the Dijon mixture. Bake until the salmon is just cooked through, 25 minutes. Broil until the top is browned, about 1 minute. Serve sprinkled with a little more fresh parsley and dill.

Fish Dish

SERVES 6

....

4 ounces slab bacon, diced

2 tablespoons extra-virgin olive oil,
plus more for drizzling

1 pound skinless firm white fish,
such as cod or halibut, cut into 12 pieces

1 pound large shrimp, peeled and deveined

Kosher salt

1 bunch leeks, white and green parts,
halved and sliced

6 cloves garlic, sliced

2 teaspoons chopped fresh thyme

¼ teaspoon crushed red pepper flakes

½ cup dry white wine

2 tablespoons red wine vinegar

1 (28-ounce) can whole plum tomatoes,
crushed by hand

1 (8-ounce) bottle clam juice

1½ pounds new potatoes, cut into 1-inch wedges

½ cup chopped fresh Italian parsley

1 loaf crusty bread

....

Plain and simple, it's fish on Friday in our family, don't ask me why. It's just what we do in our little town.

The sauce this dish creates is great for dunking! Sometimes I toast the slices of the crusty bread with a little butter and garlic spread on top. Garlic breath galore! David loves it!

HEAT A LARGE Dutch oven over medium-high heat. Add the bacon and olive oil and cook until the bacon renders its fat, about 3 minutes. Pat the fish and shrimp dry and season with salt. Add the fish to the pot and brown on all sides, about 2 minutes, and carefully transfer to a plate. Do the same with the shrimp, leaving just the bacon behind in the pot.

Once the fish and the shrimp are browned, add the leeks, garlic, and thyme to the pot and cook, stirring occasionally, until the leeks are wilted, about 6 minutes. Add the red pepper flakes then the white wine and vinegar. Bring to a simmer and cook until reduced by half, about 2 minutes. Add the tomatoes, clam juice, and 1 cup water. Bring to a simmer, add the potatoes, and season with salt. Simmer uncovered until the potatoes are tender, about 13 minutes. The stew should be thick and flavorful; if not, increase the heat and boil a few minutes to reduce and thicken the cooking juices, stirring so the potatoes don't stick to the bottom.

Add back the fish and shrimp, along with the parsley. Simmer until the seafood is just cooked through, about 3 minutes. Adjust the seasoning with salt, drizzle with a little olive oil, and stir. Serve with chunks of crusty bread for dipping.

Humble Ham Casserole

SERVES 6 TO 8

3 tablespoons unsalted butter
(plus more for the baking dish)

2 medium leeks, white and light green
parts, thinly sliced

1 tablespoon chopped fresh thyme

¼ cup all-purpose flour

2 cups milk

1 cup half-and-half

Pinch freshly grated nutmeg

Kosher salt

Freshly ground black pepper

3 medium russet potatoes (about 2 pounds),
peeled and thinly sliced

2 cups (8 ounces) shredded medium-sharp
Cheddar cheese

2 cups diced leftover baked ham

2 tablespoons dried breadcrumbs

¼ cup grated Parmesan cheese

We all know how much I love leftovers! This casserole is delicious made with leftovers from my Tavern Ham on page 47, which is so decadent that it gives the dish a head start on flavor.

My mother called this Scalloped Potatoes and Ham. I call it Humble Ham because it's a less prestigious piece of meat, but it's an old rustic farmhouse staple.

PREHEAT THE OVEN to 400°F. Butter a shallow 3-quart baking dish. In a medium saucepan, melt the butter over medium heat. Add the leeks and thyme and cook, stirring occasionally, until the leeks are softened, about 5 minutes. Sprinkle with the flour and stir and cook for 2 minutes. Whisk in the milk and half-and-half, bring to a simmer, and cook until thickened, about 5 minutes. Season with the nutmeg, salt, and pepper.

Spread about a cup of the sauce in the bottom of the buttered baking dish. Layer with half of the potatoes, half of the Cheddar, and all of the ham. Spread with another cup of sauce. Layer the rest of the potatoes over the top, then add the rest of the sauce. Sprinkle with the remaining Cheddar cheese and the breadcrumbs and Parmesan.

Cover with foil and bake until the potatoes are just tender, 35 to 40 minutes. Uncover and bake until the top is browned and bubbly, 15 to 20 minutes. Let sit for 10 minutes before serving.

Chunky Chicken Thighs
and Wild Rice

SERVES 6

2 tablespoons unsalted butter

1 tablespoon extra-virgin olive oil

1 pound boneless, skinless chicken thighs, cut into 1-inch chunks

Kosher salt

Freshly ground black pepper

1 small onion, chopped

1 large carrot, chopped

1 large stalk celery, chopped

12 ounces cremini or button mushrooms, sliced

2 quarts low-sodium chicken broth

1 tablespoon chopped fresh thyme

2 bay leaves

½ cup wild rice

1 large russet potato (about 14 ounces), peeled and chopped

½ cup heavy cream

½ cup white rice

¼ cup chopped fresh Italian parsley

This is a snow day lunch! Snow days were when my kids had to clean their rooms, and the sighs began. Sledding was always more appealing to them. This is a great meal to feed a bunch of kids after sledding—or even cleaning!

When you brown the chicken, be sure not to put too many pieces in the pan at once. If you do, the chicken will steam instead of brown, and browning is what creates those wonderful drippings that you need for flavor.

HEAT A LARGE Dutch oven over medium-high heat and add the butter and olive oil. Pat the chicken dry and season with salt and pepper. When the butter is melted, add the chicken in batches and brown all over, about 6 minutes per batch.

Add the onion, carrot, celery, and mushrooms and cook, stirring occasionally, until the mushrooms and onions are wilted, about 8 minutes. Add the broth, thyme, and bay leaves and bring to a simmer. Add the wild rice, cover, and simmer until the rice just begins to become tender, about 25 minutes (check a few times; wild rice brands can vary).

Add the potato, cream, and white rice. Simmer, uncovered, until both kinds of rice are tender, 15 to 18 minutes more. Discard the bay leaves, stir in the parsley, and serve.

Happy Holly's

Banana Cream Pie

SERVES 8

PIE DOUGH

1½ cups all-purpose flour (plus more for rolling the dough)

2 teaspoons granulated sugar

½ teaspoon kosher salt

6 tablespoons cold unsalted butter, cut into pieces

CUSTARD AND BANANAS

¾ cup granulated sugar

⅓ cup all-purpose flour

¼ teaspoon kosher salt

2 cups milk

3 large egg yolks, beaten

2 tablespoons unsalted butter

2 teaspoons vanilla extract

4 bananas, peeled

WHIPPED CREAM

1½ cups chilled heavy cream

3 tablespoons confectioners' sugar

1 teaspoon pure vanilla extract

Holly is my childhood friend and the sister I never had. She's thinner than me, naturally blond, and has the most beautiful smile. She's been in my life for 65 years. That's a long friendship—and one I feel blessed to have.

Holly's smile always makes me happy and so does her food! Boy, can she cook! Her favorite pie is banana cream and we've been making it together since we've known each other. I'm not sure whether this recipe is hers or mine!

FOR THE DOUGH, in a large bowl, combine the flour, granulated sugar, and salt. Sprinkle in the butter pieces and cut them into the flour with a pastry cutter (or 2 knives or your fingertips) until the mixture is crumbly and the pieces are the size of small peas. Mix in 5 tablespoons very cold water and toss with a fork until the dough just comes together.

Place the dough on the floured counter and knead a few times, just to make a ball. Don't overwork the dough or the crust will be tough! Lightly flour the counter. Flatten the dough into a disk and wrap in plastic. Let it rest in the refrigerator for at least 15 minutes. (If making more than 1 hour ahead, let it rest on the counter for 10 minutes before rolling out.)

Roll the dough out on a floured surface into a 12-inch circle. Fit into a 9-inch pie plate and trim to a ½-inch overhang all around. Fold the overhanging dough under itself and crimp with a fork or your fingers. Chill the pie shell in the refrigerator for 30 minutes.

Continued

Preheat the oven to 400°F. Cover the shell with a piece of parchment paper and fill with dried beans or pie weights. Bake on the bottom rack until the crust is set but still blond in color, about 20 minutes. Remove the paper and beans or weights and bake until the crust is golden brown, 10 to 15 minutes more. Let cool completely on a rack.

For the custard, in a saucepan, combine the granulated sugar, flour, and salt. Add the milk gradually while stirring. Cook over medium heat, stirring constantly, until it begins to bubble. Cook, stirring, for 3 minutes, or until it forms firm peaks.

Stir a small amount of the hot milk mixture into the beaten egg yolks in a small bowl. This will temper the yolks so they don't turn into scrambled eggs. Stir the tempered yolks back into the rest of the custard.

Cook for 2 more minutes, stirring constantly. Remove from the heat and stir in the butter and vanilla.

Slice 2 bananas into the cooled pastry crust. Top with half of the custard and slice the remaining bananas on top. Top with the rest of the custard. Chill for at least 1 hour.

For the whipped cream, in a cold bowl with an electric mixer, beat the cream, confectioners' sugar, and vanilla until firm peaks form. Be careful not to overbeat or your cream will turn to butter. Watch as you beat and stop when it gets thick and stays on the beaters when you remove them from the bowl.

Top the pie with the whipped cream and serve.

"COOKING IS LIKE LOVE. IT SHOULD BE ENTERED INTO WITH ABANDON OR NOT AT ALL."
—HARRIET VAN HORNE

Gigi's Gingerbread
with Whipped Cream:
A Forgotten Favorite

SERVES 8

GINGERBREAD

1½ cups all-purpose flour
(plus more for the baking pan)

1 teaspoon baking soda

2 teaspoons ground ginger

1 teaspoon ground cinnamon

¼ teaspoon ground cloves

¼ teaspoon freshly grated nutmeg

¼ teaspoon fine salt

½ cup (1 stick) unsalted butter, softened
(plus more for the baking pan)

½ cup granulated sugar

1 large egg

½ cup molasses

½ cup boiling water

WHIPPED CREAM

½ cup chilled heavy cream

2 tablespoons confectioners' sugar

Gingerbread was popular when I was young; we had gingerbread with whipped cream for dessert more often than we had apple pie. I had almost forgotten about this recipe, and I'm excited to make it for the holidays for my little taste testers, my grandchildren, who all call me Gigi!

When warm, the gingerbread is light and cakey—delicious. If you let it cool and cover it for half a day or so, it becomes very moist and the spicy flavor stands out even more—equally delicious but a different cake altogether. Try it both ways to see which you prefer.

FOR THE GINGERBREAD, preheat the oven to 350°F. Butter and flour an 8-inch-square baking pan and line the bottom with a square of parchment paper. Sift the flour, baking soda, ginger, cinnamon, cloves, nutmeg, and salt onto a piece of parchment paper. In a mixer fitted with the paddle attachment, beat the butter and granulated sugar on medium-high speed until light and fluffy, about 1 minute. Add the egg and beat until combined. Add the molasses and beat until combined. Reduce the speed to low and pour in the flour mixture in 3 additions, alternating with the boiling water, beginning and ending with the flour. Mix on medium high for 10 seconds, just to smooth out the batter.

Scrape the mixture into the prepared pan. Bake until a toothpick inserted into the center of the gingerbread comes out clean, 30 to 35 minutes. Cool on a rack for 15 minutes.

For the whipped cream, beat the cream in a clean mixer bowl with the whisk attachment on medium-high speed until frothy. Add the confectioners' sugar and beat until soft peaks form, about 1 minute.

Serve the squares of gingerbread with dollops of whipped cream.

Chocolate Almond-Butter Buddies

MAKES ABOUT 3½ DOZEN BUDDIES

1 cup (2 sticks) unsalted butter, softened

1 cup (about 10 ounces) almond butter

½ cup graham cracker crumbs (4 sheets)

½ teaspoon vanilla extract

4 to 4½ cups confectioners' sugar

1 (12-ounce) bag semisweet chocolate chips,
or 12 ounces chopped semisweet chocolate

1 tablespoon shortening

My son John calls *his* son John "Buddy." When I concocted this recipe I wanted to include my two boys in the name, Big John and Little John—so I named them "Buddies."

One bag of chocolate chips is *just* enough to coat one batch. If you're new to dipping candies and don't want to run out, use 1½ bags and 1½ tablespoons of shortening just to be sure you have enough.

IN A MIXER fitted with the paddle attachment, cream the butter and almond butter on medium-high speed until very smooth. Add the graham cracker crumbs and vanilla and beat again until smooth. On low speed, add 2 cups of the confectioners' sugar and beat to combine. Continue adding the sugar, about ½ cup at a time, until you can form a handful of the mixture into a slightly sticky ball. Refrigerate the dough just to firm it up a bit, 10 to 15 minutes.

Roll the dough into 1-inch balls and put on a parchment-lined baking sheet. Refrigerate until firm, about 30 minutes.

Meanwhile, melt the chocolate chips and shortening in a double boiler or a bowl set over a pan of simmering water. Stir until smooth. Remove the bowl from the heat and let the chocolate cool and thicken while the buddies chill in the refrigerator. (You want the chocolate thick enough so you can dip and coat the buddies.)

To dip them, poke a buddy with a wooden skewer or toothpick and swirl it in the melted chocolate, leaving a little of the almond butter mixture peeping out at the top. Drop it gently back onto the parchment-lined pan. Once you've dipped all of the buddies, refrigerate them until the chocolate is set, about 30 minutes.

Custard and Crust

SERVES 6 TO 8

CRUST

11 sheets graham crackers

3 tablespoons light brown sugar

5 tablespoons unsalted butter, melted and cooled (plus a little for the pie plate)

CUSTARD

¾ cup sugar

¾ cup cream

Peeled zest and 6 tablespoons juice from 2 lemons

4 large eggs

Pinch fine salt

Kids love the graham cracker crust in this simple pie and of course, the sugar! Some things never change!

I enjoy serving this with fresh berries if I can find them out of season, or a simple berry compote from berries I froze earlier in the year.

FOR THE CRUST, preheat the oven to 350°F and set a rack in the middle. Brush a 9-inch pie plate with a bit of melted butter. In a food processor, pulse the graham crackers to fine crumbs. In a medium bowl, stir together the crumbs and brown sugar with a fork until thoroughly combined. Drizzle in the 5 tablespoons melted butter to coat all of the crumbs evenly and stir with a fork to combine. Press the crumbs onto the bottom and up the sides of the pie plate. Bake on the middle rack until the crust is crisp, about 12 minutes. Cool completely on a rack.

For the custard, combine the sugar, cream, and lemon zest strips in a small saucepan. Bring to a simmer over low heat, stirring to dissolve the sugar. Simmer very gently for 5 minutes. Remove from the heat and discard the lemon strips.

In a large bowl, whisk the eggs and salt until smooth. Pour in the hot cream in a slow, steady stream, whisking the whole time. Whisk in the 6 tablespoons lemon juice.

Pour the custard into the crust. Bake until the edges are set but the center is still just a little jiggly, 25 to 30 minutes. Cool completely on a rack, then refrigerate until completely set, at least 3 hours.

Farm Family Favorite
Chocolate Cream Pie

SERVES 8

35 chocolate sandwich cookies
(such as Oreos)

4 tablespoons unsalted butter,
melted and cooled

1 half gallon chocolate ice cream,
softened at room temperature
for 15 minutes

1 cup prepared fudge sauce

1 cup heavy cream

2 tablespoons confectioners' sugar

½ teaspoon vanilla extract

2 tablespoons chocolate chips or
chocolate shavings, for garnish

I made this chocolaty ice cream pie when the kids were young and they would fight over every last morsel! Since it is such a crowd-pleaser, make it a day ahead to take to a party. The recipe calls for store-bought cookies, so it's very easy to quickly put together. Whip, whip, that's it! You can use extra Chosen Chocolate Sauce (page 58) or any prepared fudge sauce that's in the refrigerator.

IN A FOOD processor (or a large resealable plastic bag with a rolling pin), crush 25 of the cookies to fine crumbs (to get 2½ cups crumbs). Dump the crushed cookies into a large bowl. Process or smash the remaining 10 cookies into bigger chunks and set aside. To the finely crushed cookies, drizzle in the melted butter and stir with a fork to combine. Press onto the bottom and up the sides of a 9-inch deep-dish pie plate. Freeze for 30 minutes.

In a large bowl, stir together the remaining coarsely crushed cookies and the ice cream. Spread into the frozen crust, making an even layer. Freeze 30 minutes just to firm up the ice cream again.

Drizzle the frozen pie with the fudge sauce and spread in an even layer. Return to the freezer while you whip the cream.

With a handheld mixer, beat the cream until frothy. Add the confectioners' sugar and vanilla and beat until soft peaks form. Mound the whipped cream on the pie, sprinkle with the chocolate chips or chocolate shavings, and freeze until firm all the way through, about 4 hours or overnight. Use a knife dipped into hot water to cut into slices and serve.

Mind Your Manners

"FAMILIAR CHILDHOOD TASTES GIVE US A PLACE TO BELONG: THEY BEAR WITNESS TO OUR LIVES."
—MONICA BHIDE

MANNERS MAKETH THE MAN

Sitting down to dinner with your family is just about the most important thing you can do at the end of the day, and proper manners are of utmost importance when you gather around the table. When I was raising my six children, having dinner together was mandatory. Each member of my family had their own cloth napkin and pewter napkin ring with their initials engraved on it! Today, my grandchildren use their parents' napkin rings. It's a tradition in our family. You can adopt this one or create your own—whatever gets them to the table!

As I was growing up, we stood behind our chairs at the dinner table until my mother sat down. Then, everyone sat down and put their napkin on their lap, and no one picked up their fork until my mother picked up her fork and began to eat. That is just the way it was! My mother's mother taught her proper manners, my mother taught me, and I taught my children. And now, I'm teaching my grandchildren.

I have two stories, one mine and the other from my eldest child, Abby, that really demonstrate the importance of manners. First, here is mine: I was about 16 years old when my great-aunt Jo gave me a bracelet for Christmas. She had always given me a gift, and each year I had always written a thank-you note, prompted by my mother. The year of the bracelet I forgot to write her a thank-you note—and I never received another gift. It's something I've never forgotten, and it was a lesson well learned! Thank-you notes are just so important. If someone cares enough about you to give you a gift, out of respect alone, you thank that person for caring about you. Everyone wants to be cared for!

And Abby remembers being rude to guests in our home who had come for dinner many years ago: "When they left, you made me call them and apologize. This was hard to do, but I did it and they appreciated it. It's something I've never forgotten."

Manners make your first impression and keep you in the good graces of others. If practicing manners is new for you, rest assured that it's never too late to learn. When it comes to manners, you can always teach old dogs new tricks!

"IF YOU TEACH A CHILD THE RIGHT WAY TO EAT FOOD, THEY WILL GROW UP EATING THE RIGHT FOOD."
—ALICE WATERS

1.

Always sit down at the dinner table.

2.

It all begins with a napkin.

3.

At the table, always behave and sit still. Do not get up to take a phone call during dinner. And don't let your kids run around.

4.

Put your napkin on your lap as soon as you are seated at the dinner table.

5.

Always sit up straight. When eating, be sure to raise your fork to your mouth. Do not lean down to your plate.

6.

Mable, Mable, strong and able, keep your elbows off the table.

7.

Never start eating until the hostess has
picked up her fork.

....

8.

Never smell your food! Don't take a forkful
of food and put it up to your nose
and smell it.

....

9.

Never use a knife to cut a roll.
Always tear a piece of bread or roll in a size
that will fit in your mouth.

....

10.

Never butter an entire piece of bread
or roll at one time.

11.

When eating your soup, always bring the spoon to the
back of the bowl, then to your mouth.

12.

When cutting your food, cut only the bite you are putting in your mouth at that time.

14.

Never speak with food in your mouth.

15.

When wiping your mouth, fold the napkin over your index finger and wipe one corner of your mouth at a time.

16.

Always say, "Excuse me, please," when getting up from the table during dinner.

17.

When leaving the table during the meal, always lay your napkin on your seat.

13.

Always place the knife and fork at the top of the plate when resting between bites.

18.

Always push your chair under the table when you leave the table.

21.

Always place your utensils at the four o'clock position on your plate to indicate that you are through eating.

19.

Always ask to be excused when you want to leave the table after dinner. Kids should ask, "May I please be excused?"

20.

Always put your napkin next to your plate when you leave the table after you've finished your dinner.

26.

You never get a second chance to make a first impression.

....

27.

Always say "yes"; never say "yeah."

....

28.

Do not allow your children to talk back. My mother always said, "Do not contradict me."

....

29.

Always say "please" and "thank you."

....

30.

Always shake a person's hand when being introduced.

....

31.

Always respect your elders.

....

32.

Always take responsibility for your actions.

22.

Always write a thank-you note if you have attended a dinner party or have received a gift. If you're sending a thank-you note for an overnight visit, you address it to only the woman of the house.

....

23.

You may put one elbow on the table after your dessert plate has been removed.

....

24.

You are only as good as your word.

....

25.

If you have nothing to hide, you have nothing to fear.

Index

About the Author

NANCY FULLER was born on a farm in the Hudson Valley of New York State. She learned to walk by holding on to her grandmother's apron strings and hasn't strayed far from the kitchen since then. Early married life found her cooking three meals a day for a combined family of eight—perfect training for the life of a caterer. Fittingly, the farm girl's first gig was catering a cattle sale cocktail party. Her last gig was twenty-five years later. After meeting and marrying her husband, David Ginsberg, she hung up her white shirt and black bow tie and invested in his family's multimillion-dollar food distribution business where she is currently executive vice president. A champion of Hudson Valley foods, Nancy came to the attention of the Food Network while arranging to supply a locally raised pig for an independent video. The result is her show, *Farmhouse Rules*. The "all-American" grandmother of thirteen is a tireless promoter of fresh food, family values, and (mostly) good clean fun. She learned to drive a tractor before she took driver's ed.